Eats, Poops & Leaves

ALSO BY ADAM WASSON
The Self-Destruction Handbook:
8 Simple Steps to an Unhealthier You
(with Jessica Stamen)

EATS, POOPS & LEAVES

*The Essential Apologies, Rationalizations,
and Downright Denials Every
New Parent Needs to Know
and Other Fundamentals
of Baby Etiquette*

ADAM WASSON

With Illustrations by Evan Oremland

THREE RIVERS PRESS
New York

Library of Congress Cataloging-in-Publications Data

Wasson, Adam.
Eats, poops & leaves : the essential apologies, rationalizations, and downright
denials every new parent needs to know and other fundamentals of baby
etiquette / Adam Wasson ; with illustrations by Evan Oremland.—1st ed.
Includes bibliographical references.
1. Infants—Humor.   2. Child rearing—Humor.   I. Title: Eats, poops,
and leaves.   II. Title.
PN6231.I5W37 2005
818'.607—dc22   2004028614

ISBN 1–4000–9753–3

Printed in the United States of America

Design by Debbie Glasserman

10 9 8 7 6 5 4 3 2 1

First Edition

To my sweet Ava Jane
and also, of course,
to her mom, Lael

[First etiquette rule for husbands—never, ever say something nice about your daughter without also acknowledging your wife]

CONTENTS

ACKNOWLEDGMENTS

I'd like gratefully to acknowledge Stephanie Hemphill, without whose help this book would never have gotten finished; Alan Nevins, for believing I'm funny and helping me make a living at it; Mindy Stone, for keeping Alan from losing it completely; Julia Pastore, for her cleverness, honesty, and willingness to breathe new life into deadlines; and the wonderful copyeditors at Three Rivers Press, for dealing with innumerable comma splices as well as my tendency to hyphenate half cocked (or is it half-cocked?). I'd also like to thank Anne Garefino, Jessica Stamen, and Carrie Buse, whose hilarious perspectives as friends of the parent were essential to the planning and execution of the book, and the incomparable Lael Loewenstein for being, well, Lael Loewenstein. Finally, I'd like to implicate all four of my parents (Fran, Jan, Barbara, and John) and all four of my parents-in-law (Louis, Neyde, Malcolm, and Marcella). You taught me that there are many ways to parent, and that all of them are at least a little absurd.

Eats, Poops & Leaves

INTRODUCTION

You know them. The mother who seems blithely oblivious to the fact that her screaming child is terrorizing an entire airplane. The father who stumbles over startled sunbathers in a compulsive attempt to film his baby ingesting sand. Yes, you know them all right, and at some point in your life, you have despised them. These parents, you used to think to yourself, have no manners whatsoever, no clue how to interact appropriately with the outside world. They ought to be quarantined, forbidden to mix with the rest of society until they learn some civility. The problem, of course, is that now these parents are you.

That's right. Suddenly you are the person holding up the line at the grocery store, the person responsible for that suspicious stain on your cousin's new sofa. What, you wonder, is the appropriate thing to do in such a situation? Should you own up to the stain or surreptitiously attempt to cover it with a pillow? If other children are present, might you try to frame one of them? Unfortunately, there is no rule book dedicated to answering such questions—no guide that explains whether tipping your anesthesiologist will ensure an adequate epidural, no book that tells you what to do when your child shrieks at a wedding or vomits on the person standing next to you at Bloomingdale's. That is, there *was* no such book until now.

Eats, Poops & Leaves is your guide to navigating the awkward, embarrassing, and emotionally treacherous social terrain that those involved with new babies must face every day. In addition to consulting a wide variety of parents and grandparents, we have also interviewed experts in a broad range of fields—from maître d's and wedding coordinators to pediatricians and couples' therapists—in order to give you etiquette tips for both bizarre and mundane real-life situations.

Of course, new parents are not the only ones involved in maintaining good baby etiquette. There are also many friends and family members who must deal regularly with new parents and their offspring. With that in mind, we have included special "Friends and Family" boxes that speak to the etiquette needs of those closest to new parents. What are the best and worst baby gifts? How do you tell a new parent you don't want their baby's slobbering maw within twenty yards of your valuable antiques? What should you do if your best friend consults you on the issue of naming his first child "Morpheus"?

The answers to all of the above questions, and to hundreds of others, await you in the following pages. Whether you are a prospective parent planning to purloin a friend's pet baby name, or a single parent hoping to milk some cash out of sympathetic relatives, the point of *Eats, Poops & Leaves* is to offer everyone involved with new babies an innovative and humorous guide to interacting with the nonbaby world around them.

1

Beyond Aubrey and Ashlee

Naming Etiquette

WHAT'S IN A NAME?

Issues of baby etiquette can surface even before you give birth to your child, and one of the most important is naming etiquette. The name you choose will affect not only your child, but also everyone else—from friends to teachers to significant others—who has to say your child's name in the future. With that in mind, we have listed some of the most popular and effective naming strategies below.

"Artistic" Names

For many years, "creative" child names such as Piper, Scout, Apple, and Phinnaeus were primarily the province of pretentious Hollywood actors. Since the American middle class has risen in affluence and feelings of self-consequence, however, there is really no reason for anyone to forego the pleasure of giving their child an artistic name.

The secret to "creating" a good name is to let your mind go completely blank, as though it is a clean, bare tablet unencumbered by intelligence or taste. Then, once your brain is utterly empty, name your child the first thing that pops into your head. Pear, January, Studebaker—the weirder the name, the greater its "artistic" statement.

Place Names

Currently, the most fashionable naming strategy is to give your child a location rather than a name—Brooklyn, for example, or Ireland.

E T I Q U E T T E   T I P
When picking a place-name, it is best
to stick with first-world locations (Kuala Lumpur does not
carry quite the same social cache as, say, Venice).

Ultimately, the point of a good place-name is to grant your child a sense of self-importance well before they've achieved anything on their own. With luck, your child will live up to this glamorous image, and one day may even outstrip their namesake in global notoriety.

Paris Hilton currently has a higher recognition factor among teenage Americans than does Paris, France.

Adding Es to a Name

If you want the comfort of a popular name but would like to add a splash of creativity, try taking a name that ends in *Y* and end it instead with *EE*. Ashlee, for instance, instead of Ashley. If you feel that this is not unique enough, go ahead and add more Es. There may be another Ashlee or two in your daughter's class, but she will most likely be the only Ashleeeee.

Stripper Names

If you would like your child to become a stripper, it is best to pick pseudosexy names such as Misty, Savannah, Essence, or Cherry Pie. If you've already chosen a normal name but think you might want your child to be a stripper, you can always consider replacing the last vowel in the name with "ique." Monique and Angelique, for instance, make excellent stripper names, as does Larrique for a boy.

There has never been a stripper named Eunice.

WHY ADDING "LE" OR "LA" TO A NAME DOES NOT ACTUALLY MAKE IT MORE CLASSY

Adding French articles to American names—LaDonna, for instance, or DeShawn for a boy—has long been a way for everyday Americans to indicate a certain cosmopolitan sophistication. Since our break with the French over issues of foreign policy, however, such naming strategies have become less, shall we say, au courant. The good news is that these unpatriotic French articles are quickly being replaced by the addition of genuine American articles. Today, for instance, if you want your son to be very successful, it is an excellent idea to name him "The Donald" instead of just Donald.

Fanciful Boy Names

One time-tested way for young boys to build character is to be humbled and even, occasionally, physically assaulted by other kids. These experiences instill an inner resolve, a desire to escape or surpass one's peers that can ultimately result in great professional success. A good way to ensure that your son gets this kind of head start is to allow your wife to name him without any kind of masculine supervision. Aubrey, Tristan, and Remi are all good examples of fanciful names; Avery, Gideon, and Puck should also elicit a few blows to the head during your son's formative years.

Annoying Names

Occasionally, new parents want a baby name that will be just plain annoying to friends, family, and nearly everyone else with whom your child comes into contact. In this case, it is a good idea to name your child after an already overexposed celebrity or literary figure. Holden, for instance, makes an excellent annoying boy name, as does Britney for a little girl.

Seeking Advice

Most people like the idea of discussing potential baby names with people they trust, and it is understandable that you want help and reassurance in making such a momentous decision.

Remember, though, that your most considerate friends will not tell you directly what they think about a name, so you will have to read between the lines in order to divine their true opinion. The following table should give you some idea how the naming double-talk works.

THE NAME GAME

WHAT FRIENDS SAY	TRANSLATION
"That's nice."	"Boring."
"Interesting."	"Hate it."
"What a beautiful name."	"What a beautiful name."
"You're so creative."	"Oh. My. God. That is heinous."
"Oooh, I love that name!"	"Hmm . . . I might steal that name."
"Really? I knew a . . . once."	"I'm a narcissist and not at all interested in what you name your baby."

Name Stealing

Suppose that you are out at a dinner party full of prospective parents, and one of the other parents makes the mistake of letting an enticing prospective baby name slip. There are three questions to ask yourself when preparing to purloin the name:

1. Do you actually care about the individuals in question? You may have a few friends in common, but honestly, would it bother you at all to incur the wrath and lifetime enmity of these people? If not, go ahead and poach that name.

2. Can they be bought? It is possible that these people are in financial difficulty and could be bribed into giving up the name.

3. Would your child be able to "take" their child? Make an honest survey of your physical gifts as a couple—height, strength, punching power, etc.—and try to estimate how your child would one day fare in a physical altercation with his or her unwilling namesake. If the answer is "not well," you may want to consider a different name.

Baby Nicknames

At least for the first few years, your baby's actual name will be almost irrelevant—she will be referred to instead by a variety of nicknames. There are reputations and fortunes to be made on baby nicknames that stick—Tiger Woods, for example, would probably not have a hundred-million-dollar Nike contract were he referred to as Eldrick—so do not take this task lightly.

The trap most parents fall into is relying on clichéd nicknames, which should be avoided at all costs. You can begin

FRIENDS AND FAMILY BOX
What If You Hate the Name?

When you dislike or are lukewarm about the name in question, a good way to avoid ill feelings is to utilize a pleasant but non-committal response. A simple but not overwarm "all right," for instance, can deliver just the right mixture of support and ambivalence. Similar semisupportive phrases include "That works," "I could see that," and "Is that a family name?"

If the name is truly ghastly, you may want to opt for a more obviously double-edged response, such as "interesting" or, in dire circumstances, "wow." To anyone who actually wants your opinion, this makes it fairly clear that you loathe the name. But for those who are simply determined to go with a bad name, such a response allows you to avoid giving offense while nonetheless withholding any real approbation.

your cliché cleansing by abolishing all uses of the word "Boo," whether in its singular, doubled, or compound forms. Boo, Boo-Boo, and Petey-Boo are all different and all equally lame. Try also to stay away from the "Four Ps" of clichéd nicknaming: Peanut, Pumpkin, Precious, and Princess.

Instead, see if you can come up with a nickname that is in some way indicative of your child's character: Gobbles, Screech, Pukie, The Little General, Sobs-a-Lot, and The Enemy of All Sleep are all good examples of personalized nicknames.

Hyphenated Last Names

When both members of a couple keep their family names, there will inevitably be a debate as to what the baby's last name should be. The most obvious compromise is to hyphenate the last name, but this is a good time to remember that baby etiquette extends also to the babies themselves and that it is ultimately the child who will grow up and have to fill out DMV forms with a name like Anastasia Bugatti-Saperstein, have Bugatti-Saperstein on the back of her basketball jersey, and perhaps most difficult of all, have to introduce herself as "Bugatti-Saperstein" thousands upon thousands of times. Sometimes it's best just to pick a name and go with it.

2

Born Free (Minus Deductible)

Birth Etiquette

PREPARING FOR THE BIRTH
Birth Classes

Birth classes such as Lamaze are an essential part of your pre-birth preparation, because they help you get past your anxiety about the birth process. The theory behind these classes is simple: After spending hours crammed into uncomfortable chairs, making **awkward conversation** to strangers with whom you have nothing in common other than a swelling belly and an incipient sense of existential panic, birth itself will seem like a vacation.

Awkward Birth-Class Conversation Tip for Men:
Pretend to Listen, Respond

There is a good chance that you will be thinking about work, stressing about finances, and/or mourning your lost youth and thus will not even hear what another prospective father is saying

BREATHING EXERCISES

Breathing exercises are an integral part of birth-preparation classes. While they do nothing to minimize pain or stress during delivery, the sight of multiple yuppies huffing and puffing in unison does provide a mildly entertaining spectacle for the class instructor.

to you. In this case, a good strategy is to shake your head bemusedly and repeat the word "unbelievable" whenever it is your turn to speak. "How about this weather?" "Unbelievable." "Lakers look good this year." "Unbelievable." "So, you guys are having twins?" "Unbelievable." "Unbelievable" is currently the most popular word in awkward father-to-father interactions, easily outdistancing the utilitarian but less-inspired "huh," "no kidding," and "you got that right."

Awkward Birth-Class Conversation Tip for Women: Cattily Compare Your Unborn Children

It is never too early for mothers to begin comparing their children, and birth-preparation classes provide an ideal opportunity to see how your unborn child measures up. Such *in utero* comparisons are a delicate skill, however—a bit like playing a hand of bridge when you are unsure of your opponent's cards. Try whenever possible to lead with a question, which will give you time to assess your antagonist's strengths and weaknesses before making a definitive move.

EXAMPLE:

Mom #1: Do you ever play any of that womb-music?

Mom #2: Well, she's been listening to some Mozart in the womb. You wouldn't believe how much she responds to it.

Mom #1: Actually, I would. Mine used to kick like crazy with Mozart, but now he's moved into a Mahler phase—I seriously can't believe how sophisticated his tastes are.

Analysis: This exchange was brilliantly played by Mom #1, as she led with a seemingly innocent question but closed on an authoritative statement that left little room for rebuttal. The mistake Mom #2 made was in answering the question as posed. Rather than responding to the question, which put her immediately in a vulnerable position, she instead should have trumped Mom #1's first question by turning it against her.

EXAMPLE:

Mom #1: Do you ever play any of that womb-music?

Mom #2: Actually, I've heard that singing to your child is much better, because their brains are stimulated by the melodies, but the sound of your voice also makes them feel calm and loved.

Analysis: Now it is Mom #1 who is on the defensive. She can either persist in her strong suit of Mahler womb-music, which would make her seem like an unfeeling mother concerned only with superficial accomplishments, or she can pretend to be interested in Mom #2's point and follow up on it. Even if she does so, however, Mom #2 will still have the advantage of final word.

EXAMPLE:

Mom #1: Right, singing to them—I've heard that, too! Fortunately, my husband was a lead in his college choir, and he sings lullabies into my belly every night.

Mom #2: That's so wonderfull—he must have a great voice! My husband isn't much of a singer, but he's close friends with Glenn Frey. Glenn comes over a couple times a week, and oh my gosh, you should feel her kick during "Seven Bridges Road."

Analysis: Mom #1 makes a clever segue here from baby comparison into husband comparison, but Mom #2 is not rattled, and she closes out the exchange with authority. Although Mom #2 may have gone a bit over the top with her Glenn Frey reference, remember that there is a good chance she won't see any of these people again, and thus her untruth will forever go undetected.

ETIQUETTE TIP
Lying egregiously can be one of the most entertaining ways to get through the tedium of birth-preparation classes.

Showing the Sonogram Picture

Before giving birth, it is important to prepare yourself for one of the most fundamental duties of parenthood—the forcing of pictures upon a semienthusiastic audience. When you receive your first sonogram pictures, make sure to **e-mail copies** to friends and family, and print out a wallet-sized picture you can show to acquaintances and even, upon occasion, complete strangers.

FRIENDS AND FAMILY BOX
What to Say When Your Pregnant Friend Shows You a Sonogram Picture

Wow. That's really just . . . wow.
What an adorable nose! Oh, that's your cervix? Well, what an adorable cervix!
She looks like . . . your mom?

Packing for the Hospital

A common mistake made by moms-to-be is overpacking for the hospital. Most hospitals are well supplied with water, for instance, so that is not something you need to bring with you. Hospitals also have toilet paper, tissue, blankets, pillows, and food (that said, the food is generally not edible, so you might do well to pack some). Food notwithstanding, however, nearly all of the things in that bag are probably unnecessary. Psychiatrists who study prenatal psychology believe that this manic overpacking is closely related to the *nesting impulse*.

THE "NESTING" IMPULSE

A day or two before going into labor, some women will feel compelled to collect mud and dry twigs and fashion them into a crude treetop abode. The "nesting" impulse is a perfectly natural phenomenon and is nothing to worry about.

THE DELIVERY
Who Gets to Be in the Delivery Room?

One of the most difficult etiquette questions for moms-to-be is, "Who gets to be in the delivery room?" While this issue can sometimes result in hurt feelings and/or family power struggles, do try to remember that this is **your day,** and in the end, you should have only people in the room whom you love and trust—plus, of course, your husband.

This list of intimates will generally include:

Husband (if you are married; otherwise, not)
Mom

Sister

Sister's bizarre friend Liz, with whom she's staying because apparently you don't have enough room in your house; whatever, it's not like she's asking for a suite or anything, and why shouldn't mom stay in a hotel room?

Doctor

Nurse

Husband's sound guy

And, to keep you calm through all of this, you may also want to include a birth doula.

DOULA FAQS

What Is a Doula?
A doula is someone with expertise in alternative birth techniques who allows overprivileged people to feel they are having a better birth "experience."

How Do I Use My Doula?
First of all, it is important to say "my doula" as often as possible. The phrase "my doula" is what the phrase "my BMW" used to be. Draw out the first vowel just a little bit for emphasis: "My dooo-la." Go ahead and give it a try. Satisfying, no?

Where Can I Find a Good Doula?
Either through word of mouth or on websites such as 2pregnant2rich.com

Men: Videotaping the Birth

Before videotaping the birth, it is helpful to ask yourself one very important question: Will anyone ever, under any possible circumstance, want to watch this tape? If the answer is no, you may want to forego the camera and focus instead on comforting your partner.

If the answer is somehow yes, there are three basic rules of delivery-room film etiquette that all prospective fathers should follow.

1. Avoid giving directions such as, "Look into the camera, honey," or "Doc, could you try to look a little more intense?" Think of yourself more as a documentarian than as an actual director.
2. Avoid any and all close-ups. Your wife will thank you.
3. If you feel the need to hire a sound guy (and really, if you're going to do it right, you need professional sound), make sure he's got a long boom mike so that he doesn't get caught in the frame and/or interfere with the medical procedure.

Women: Should I Have an Epidural?

This is a highly personal choice that all women must make for themselves. If you cannot make up your mind whether or not to have an epidural, try answering the diagnostic questions below.

1. Do you enjoy pain?
2. Do you live in the nineteenth century?

If you answered no to the above questions, then an epidural is probably a good choice. Note: While there is currently no proof that tipping your anesthesiologist will result in a stronger epidural, there is anecdotal evidence to suggest that slapping your forearm and begging for "some serious juice" can occasionally result in a more generous dosage.

Pain Etiquette

Even women who do opt for an epidural can experience prolonged, intense pain during labor and childbirth. Pain, unfortunately, is generally not conducive to tactful conversation, so it is a good idea to have responses already prepared for the inane questions people (i.e., husbands) will inevitably ask you.

Q: How are you feeling?
A: Like a human head is being forced through my vaginal canal. How about yourself?

Q: How's the pain?
A: Top-notch, thanks.

Q: I wish I could share the pain with you.
A: That would be so great, honey! Let's stick a bowling ball up your . . .

Q: Can I get anything for you?
A: How about a vasectomy?

THE RECOVERY
Enjoy Feeling Special

Enjoy this day! You have accomplished a miraculous thing, and everyone wants to celebrate and take care of you for one last day before you begin that long, slogging journey into motherhood. From tomorrow forward, your life will be a study in sacrifice and self-abnegation, your needs attended to by no one. So, seriously, enjoy this day!

Learn from the Maternity Ward Nurses

The recovery period is an excellent time for you to learn from the maternity ward nurses. If you have a camera, try to get footage of a maternity nurse comforting, burping, and, most important, **swaddling** the baby.

FRIENDS AND FAMILY BOX
Words Other Than "Beautiful"
to Use When Appraising a New Baby

precious
healthy
alert
breathing
not too smushed
little hands/feet

SWADDLING TECHNIQUES

Swaddling is a practice of infant mummification that makes your child feel comfortable and safe. Unfortunately, it is an extremely difficult job that generally seems to mystify new parents. Part of the reason for this is that there is no single correct way to swaddle a baby. In addition to the traditional maternity-nurse technique, there are also some alternative methods that may come more naturally to new moms and dads.

Traditional four-point technique

1. Spread blanket in a diamond shape, laying baby in the middle (see figure 1)

Figure 1

2. Take left-hand point, pull it across and tuck behind back
3. Take right-hand point, pull it across and tuck behind back
4. Take bottom point, pull up snugly to baby's chest and tuck

Five-point technique for dads

1. Spread blanket in a diamond shape, laying baby in middle
2. Take left-hand point, pull it across and tuck behind back
3. Take a long moment to reflect on the physics of the four-point technique and decide that it won't work

4. Come up with an innovative solution (see figure 2) involving duct tape

Figure 2

5. Listen patiently as wife berates you

Six-point technique for moms

1. Spread blanket in a diamond shape, laying baby in middle
2. Faithfully follow steps two through four of nurse's technique
3. Watch blanket unravel
4. Pile on more blankets, reasoning that at least the baby won't be cold (see figure 3)

Figure 3

5. Remove blankets, fearing that baby might somehow suffocate
6. Ask husband where he put the duct tape

POSTPARTUM DEPRESSION

After a woman gives birth, there will be a phase during which she is moody, unpredictable, and sometimes just plain mean. What little energy she has will be devoted to caring for her new child, while her husband and friends will be left to cope with the emotional fallout. Fortunately for everyone involved, this phase of postpartum depression generally only lasts for the first eighteen years, after which she will return to her engaging, sexy, fun-loving self.

FRIENDS AND FAMILY BOX
Potential Response Strategies When a
New Mother Asks You, "How Do I Look?"

Comparison: Way better than that woman in 207.
Misdirection: I think these flower arrangements are gorgeous! Who sent this one?
Irony: Is that a rhetorical question?
Brutal honesty: Like a car ran over you, stopped, and then, for some horrifically sadistic reason, went into reverse and backed over you again.

DAD'S CORNER: IS IT MINE?

The moment you told your friends that your wife was pregnant, they had one overwhelming response: Is it yours? This wasn't funny at the time, and it's not funny now. But, for whatever reason, new dads are sometimes haunted by the specter of ersatz paternity, no matter how outlandish it may seem. Since this is obviously not a question you can ask your wife in any outright way, we have included a few tips to help put your mind at ease.

The Baby Is Not Yours If:

You have blood type O, and your child has blood type AB.
You first met the mother two months ago.
It bears an uncanny resemblance to Charlie Sheen.

If none of the above are true, then it is most likely your child. If you still have lingering doubts and would like to find out for certain in front of a caring, supportive studio audience, the *Jerry Springer* show will be delighted to make arrangements for more advanced testing.

3

Once Bitten, Twice Dry

Nursing Etiquette

BOTTLE OR BREAST?

People often think of nursing etiquette solely in terms of public breast-feeding, but you will soon discover that there are many other questions of nursing tact with which women have to contend. In fact, one important issue is going to arise even before you leave the hospital. The first time a maternity nurse takes your baby to the nursery, she is going to ask you THE QUESTION: Bottle or Breast?

Based on your answer, your child will be labeled with one of the following stickers:

I'm a breast-fed baby

or

My parents don't care

The pressure put on today's moms to take a breast-only approach to feeding their children can sometimes seem overwhelming. While it is true that there are benefits to breast-feeding and that most women today do choose this option, it is also true that many women cannot or simply do not want to breast-feed—at least not all the time. If you are among this group and find yourself reproached by, say, a militant member of the La Leche League, it is helpful to have a few tactful rebuttal strategies at your disposal.

"Formula" for Success
Rebuttal Strategies for Bottle-Feeding Moms

Argument: Formula is not natural
Rebuttal: Neither are computers, cars, antibiotics, or Stone Phillips. But, frankly, what would life be without them? (Stone Phillips optional)

Argument: Breast-feeding makes babies feel loved
Rebuttal: So does love

Argument: Formula is too expensive
Rebuttal: Husband getting up at 3 A.M. to fix a bottle while you keep sleeping? Priceless.

Argument: Breasts are best!
Rebuttal: After twelve months of nursing, they won't look like the best. They won't even look average. They will look like a pair of withered yams.

DADS' BOX
Breasts Are Best!

Incredibly, some dads actually promote the idea of bottle-feeding, reasoning that this will allow them to be as close to the child as moms during that first year of life. Try very hard to understand the implications of this philosophy: **3 A.M., bottle, screaming baby, you.** Children, moreover, don't even remember the first year of life. If you want to bond early with your child, feel free to start spoiling them sometime during the second year, when they are more communicative and fun. Moms will have started to fade by that time, and you will step in and save the day without having to go the first eighteen months without sleep. Remember, breasts are best—at least for you.

BREAST-FEEDING FASHIONS

One of the many difficult things for new moms is that motherhood in general, and nursing in particular, are not conducive to fashionable dress. The good news is that this is beginning to change. Designers and tastemakers are becoming increasingly aware of lactating moms as a viable fashion demographic, and as a result there are several new "nursing looks" (see figures 1–3) that should be available this fall.

The "Boob-alicious" Look

Truth be told, you probably won't get many evenings out while you are nursing. Occasionally, however, it can be fun to flaunt

Figure 1—Bitter and Exhausted

Figure 2—Cape Cod Cool

Figure 3—Sporty Spice

your newly enhanced décolletage in public. For women who grew up with small or average-sized breasts, this is the look you've always dreamed of (except for the eye bags, the hormone-related acne, and the unwanted postpregnancy pounds—in fact, now that we come to it, even the whole large-breast thing is really more your husband's dream than yours). Nevertheless, this may be your only opportunity to wear one of those sexy C-cup outfits, and you should go ahead and try it while you've got the opportunity. Just one word of warning: Watch out for that pesky "letdown reflex."

The Letdown Reflex

If you have the misfortune to hear a baby crying while you are out in public, it is possible that your breasts will begin to lactate spontaneously, dripping or even spraying milk all over your outfit. There are several possible ways to deal with this issue.

Own up to it. The most mature way to handle the situation is to say, "Excuse me, I'm lactating," and get the situation out in the open. Then the people around you will be able to feel included in the problem and may even have some helpful opinions about what to do next. Unfortunately, few women are confident enough to adopt the "own up to it" method in practice, especially with people they don't know very well.

Ignore it. If you are able to ignore the fact that your outfit is becoming drenched, it is possible that others will pretend not to notice. They will of course tell stories about it afterward, but never to your face.

Embrace the "wet look." In the same way that the "wet look" was a popular hair style among young men in the late '80s, so is the "wet-blouse look" becoming a popular style among nursing mothers who are back in the workplace or out for a night on the town. The trick here is to even out the wet spots and make them look intentional. If one breast is lactating more than the other, simply excuse yourself to the bathroom and splash water on the less prolific breast to balance out your look. If anyone in the bathroom asks what you are up to, condescendingly explain that this is the latest fashion, and encourage them to try a "dash of splash."

NURSING IN PUBLIC

For women who breast-feed their children, one of the touchiest issues has always been whether or not to nurse in public places. Most U.S. states now have laws that specifically permit women to nurse in public, so **this is not a legal issue.** You have the right to nurse wherever you want. Rather, this is a question of social etiquette and personal choice.

Our advice on the matter is as follows:

If you are modest and use a nursing blanket, anyone who objects to your actions is repressive and laden with unresolved issues, and you should feel free to ignore them.
If you decide to nurse without benefit of covering, anyone who objects to your actions is repressive and laden with unresolved issues, and you should feel free to ignore them.

In the latter case, however, you should also be prepared for the fact that there will inevitably be at least one guy who tries to sneak a peek at your exposed breast. When you catch such a pervy peeker in the act, it is important to gauge the extent of his offense before mounting your counterattack.

The Sly Glance

A single quick, curiosity-satisfying glance is one thing and should probably just be ignored. Repeated sly glances, on the

The Sly Glance

other hand, are very rude and deserving of rebuttal. If you find yourself the object of repeated glances, catch the man's eye, hold it for a long moment, and then say, "Wait'll you see the other one."

The Direct Ogle

The prolonged, direct ogle absolutely demands a vehement response. Good choices include, "Sorry, is the baby blocking your view?" and the ever popular, "Want some?"

The Direct Ogle

How to Maintain Your Dignity While Attached to a Breast Pump

Although a number of studies have been conducted on this issue, none has yet cracked the problem of how to pump in a dignified way. There is something about the industrial whine of the machine combined with the fact that you are being, well, milked. It's a degrading experience, but try to remember that this is all for a good cause—making your husband get up with that bottle in the middle of the night.

ETIQUETTE TIP

Never, ever say the word "moo" in the vicinity of a woman attached to a breast pump.

DAD'S BOX

What to Do When Your Male Friends
Catch You Wearing a "Boppy,"
or Strap-on Nursing Pillow

When you start giving your child bottles, you will quickly discover that it is much easier to do while resting the child on a foam nursing pillow. The only problem is that when you are tired and distracted, you may forget to unstrap yourself from the pillow when your friends stop by for a visit. Few things are more emasculating than greeting a male friend while wearing a nursing pillow. One possible way to "pass off" the pillow is to claim that it is an "all-purpose" tray, and as you sit down to watch the game, rest beer, chips, and remote controls on it. If you approach this ruse with confidence, it is entirely possible that your friends may want one themselves by the end of the evening.

Disguising Your Boppy

WHAT SHOULD YOU DO WHEN YOUR BABY BITES YOU?

Somewhere around the age of six months, babies begin to bite. And it hurts. When your baby bites you, and she will, there are two schools of thought on how to respond: **Old school** and **New school.**

FIRST BITE

NEW SCHOOL	OLD SCHOOL
"Honey, that really hurt Mommy. Can you try to be careful?"	"Ow! Bite me again, see what happens."

SECOND BITE

NEW SCHOOL	OLD SCHOOL
"Honey, how about if you don't bite me, then we can have an extra ten minutes of story time before bed?"	Bite back, ask, "How do you like it?"

SUBSEQUENT BITES

NEW SCHOOL	OLD SCHOOL
Contact La Leche society for advice.	Stop breast-feeding.

WEANING

This brings us to the issue of weaning your child. At some point, generally around the first birthday, you will probably want to stop breast-feeding. There are a number of strategies for weaning your child, but the three most popular are listed below.

The "cold-turkey" approach. Hand child and bottle of formula to husband and say, "Your turn." Sleep for six days. When you wake up, weaning process will be over and husband will have a much deeper appreciation of what this whole parenting thing is about.

The "tapered" approach. Currently the most common weaning strategy, the tapered approach involves replacing certain breast-feedings with solid food, gradually decreasing breast-feedings and adding solid food until weaning is complete.

The "infant-led" approach. This approach allows children to determine when they are ready to wean, a concept that is, frankly, a bit uncomfortable for everyone. Imagine your six-year-old publicly demanding "a little sugar," and you can see why the tapered approach is replacing the infant-led approach amongst polite society.

4

To Sleep, Perchance to Scheme

The Etiquette of Exhaustion

THE QUEST FOR REST

New parents are often surprised to find that, next to the baby herself, sleep has become their most jealously guarded commodity. Like drowning people struggling for air, sleep-challenged parents can sometimes become desperate in their quest for rest, saying or doing things of which they are later ashamed. The goal of this chapter is to put an end to that shame, and to help you advance your sleep-related schemes with at least a modicum of dignity and class.

Tricks of the Trade

One of the first things taught in traditional parenting manuals are "surefire" strategies for making your child fall asleep. What these manuals generally don't mention, however, are the side effects of such strategies. It is only by carefully weighing both benefits and side effects that you can accurately determine whether or not a given method is worth pursuing.

TURNING ON A BLOW-DRYER RIGHT NEXT TO THE CRIB

Benefit: Loud, continuous rushing noises are comforting to babies, and hair dryers do a good job of creating such continuous noise.

Side effects: Your electric bill will go up hundreds of dollars, and if you fall asleep with the hair dryer on, it could easily overheat and cause a fire that would destroy your entire house (and give new meaning to the term "surefire" strategy).

Analysis: Getting your child to sleep is definitely worth hundreds of dollars. Is it worth risking a burned-down house? Some would say yes, some would say no.

DRIVING THE BABY AROUND IN THE CAR

Benefit: The soothing hum and vibration of a moving car mimics a baby's movement in the womb and can be sleep-inducing.

Side effects: Once your child falls asleep in the car, he's **asleep in the car,** not in his crib.

Analysis: As long as you are willing to spend the entire night crammed into the front seat of your car, this method is useful. Otherwise it is pointless, because when you try to transfer your child from the car to his crib, he will inevitably wake up screaming.

BEGGING ABJECTLY FOR CHILD TO FALL ASLEEP

Benefit: Abject begging is free, and many people feel that its efficacy is equal to that of other "surefire" techniques.

Side effects: Some loss of dignity.

Analysis: Would you rather have sleep or dignity? That's what we thought. Go ahead and try begging.

Sleep Training

One of the greatest innovations in modern parenting, sleep training is now recommended by most pediatricians as a way of encouraging your child to get to sleep and stay asleep. There are several methods of sleep training, but far and away the most popular is called the *Ferber method*.

FERBER FAQS

Q: What is the Ferber method?

A: A regimen of sleep training in which the child is allowed to cry alone in her crib for increasingly longer periods—five minutes, ten minutes, fifteen minutes, etc.—until finally she learns to self-comfort and fall asleep on her own.

Q: Am I a bad parent for letting my child cry?

A: No, you are a bad person.

Q: Will this process damage my child emotionally?

A: No. They won't even remember it. You, however, may never recover. Those heartrending screams could echo through your unconscious for the rest of your days.

"FERBERIZING" YOUR WIFE

The process of Ferberizing your wife is not unlike that of Ferberizing your child. Within about thirty seconds of your child

starting to cry, your wife will also begin to get teary and to look
at you reproachfully as though this entire thing is your fault. It
is essential that you ignore her tears and learn to recognize the
varying stages of her distemper.

The sullen stare. The sullen stare is nothing to worry
about. It is difficult for a new mother not to rush to the rescue
when she hears her child cry, and a certain amount of unhap-
piness is normal on such occasions.

The Sullen Stare

The accusing glare. The accusing glare usually follows
the sullen stare by a minute or two and is meant to suggest that
you are somehow the architect of this excruciating situation. If
it weren't for you and your coldhearted adherence to the sleep-
training plan, the baby would not be crying. When you are
confronted with an accusing glare, try to ignore it for as long as
possible—even when it is accompanied by tears.

The Accusing Glare

The total breakdown. When your wife begins to sob louder and more vehemently than your child, she is heading for a **total breakdown** in which she will jettison the Ferber method entirely. This is the time to move in and provide comfort. Give her a hug, reassure her, tell her everything is going to work out for the best. Do whatever you have to do to keep her out of the baby's room until your child falls asleep. Once your wife sees that the Ferber method is working, she will gradually learn to self-comfort, and the entire process will go much more smoothly.

The Total Breakdown

DID YOU KNOW?
Sleep deprivation is a sophisticated and
effective form of torture practiced by the U.S. military,
the Iraqi military, the Israeli secret
service, and your child.

The Baby Monitor

While the baby herself ensures that you go sleepless while she is awake, the "baby monitor" is there to ensure that you will also remain sleepless after she goes down for the night.

The principle behind this is simple: The monitor is so sensitive that it sometimes picks up your baby's breathing noises; other times, it does not. When the baby shifts to a position from which you can no longer hear her on the monitor, the *overanxious parent* will begin to fear that their child is no longer breathing at all.

When you are the *less anxious parent,* it is important to remain calm when holding a conversation about whether or not your child is still breathing.

EXAMPLE

"Is the baby breathing?"

"I assume so. Is there some reason he wouldn't be?"

"I can't hear him breathing!"

"You can't hear your mother breathing, either."

"My mother's in San Francisco."

"Exactly. Do you want me to fly there and check on her, or can we assume that even though we don't hear her breathing, she's doing it anyway?"

"I see your point. So, are you going to check on the baby or should I?"

"I'll do it."

[Five-minute hiatus while you check on the baby]

"The baby's fine."

"I'm worried about my mother."

The Breathing Check

One of the most difficult maneuvers in all of parenting, the breathing check can be broken down into three distinct phases: **opening the door, approaching the crib,** and **reassuring yourself that the baby is breathing.**

Phase 1: Open the door. The trick with opening the door is to do it quickly and firmly. Moving too slowly can actually cause more creaks, and the longer the noisy period, the greater the chance your child will waken and begin crying. Remember when opening the door to put on your **door-opening face** (see figure 1).

Phase 2: Silently approach the crib. The crib-approach is a vital yet often neglected skill: Most unsuccessful breathing checks are bungled on the approach. There are two distinct

Figure 1

styles to consider when preparing to make your approach: the *Indian Walk* and the *Abject Slither*.

The Indian Walk is a confident, almost spiritual approach. In bare feet, move across the floor as smoke caresses feathers, as wind dances over the plains of your ancestors.

For those not quite spiritual enough to attempt an Indian Walk, your best bet is the Abject Slither. Crawl on your belly to the edge of the crib and then slowly, silently, pull yourself up to a standing position.

Phase 3: Obtain breathing reassurance. With luck, your child will be breathing loudly enough that you can hear it from close range and return to bed reassured. If not, however, you will need to go with a poke-check.

The poke-check consists of a gentle nudge with the index finger to your child's arm or leg. The idea is to disturb the baby just enough that she will shift, groan, or exhale without fully waking up. The chances are high that the poke-check will waken her completely and occasion a prolonged bout of shrieking, but at least the shrieking will reassure you that she is, in fact, still breathing.

MIDDLE-OF-THE-NIGHT-WAKE-UP ETIQUETTE

There are many ways of addressing the issue of who gets up in the middle of the night. One way is to alternate nights, another is to alternate weeks. Yet another common method is to assign night duty on the basis of who has more important things to do the next day.

DID YOU KNOW?
During his first year of fatherhood,
the average man's number of
"important next-day meetings" goes up 302 percent.

For many couples, though, the terms of who gets up in the middle of the night are never entirely clarified. In this case, the best way to make a determination is to **engage in a passive-aggressive battle of wills.** There are a number of weapons that can be used in this struggle, and some of the most effective are listed below.

POTENTIAL WEAPONS IN A PASSIVE-AGGRESSIVE BATTLE OF WILLS

The Angelic Slumber. If the baby begins screaming and you are relatively sure your partner is awake, one popular strategy is to feign a peaceful, angelic slumber. If your partner sees you so placidly composed, they may not have the heart to awaken you.

The Insensible Grunt. One essential thing in this battle of wills is that **you do not speak first.** Coherent speech indicates that you are awake, and thus fully capable of attending to your child. If your partner knows you are awake and says something to the effect of, "You up?" your best bet is to answer with an insensible grunt. This says, "Yes, I'm awake but so foggy as to be incapable of speech. Do you really want me picking up the baby in this handicapped state?"

The Hard Stare. When both of you are startled from a deep slumber and neither has the capacity to feign sleep, the hard stare can be an effective stratagem. The trick here is to fix your partner with a calm, unwavering gaze that says, "I know you're awake, you know you're awake, and we both know that it's your turn." It is a rare combatant who will not wilt under a determined hard stare.

Sending the Baby on a "Wake-up" Mission

If you are outmaneuvered in the opening passive-aggressive battle, do not despair. Remember as you change that diaper and administer the bottle that you are now holding the ultimate weapon in the sleep wars—**the baby herself.** To deploy this weapon, simply carry the baby to the bed and place her warm, fuzzy head into a nuzzling position on the neck of your slumbering partner. There is an excellent chance that the baby's unadulterated cuteness will coerce your partner out of sleep. They will not be able to resist a prolonged bout of baby nuzzling, and you will thus be freed to exit the room and catch a nice nap on the couch.

HOW LATE CAN FRIENDS CALL?

Occasionally, single friends with whom you used to carouse will call you after 10 P.M. just to "say hi" or "see what's up." You can take out some of your pent-up, sleep-deprived, midlife-crisis frustration on these friends in one of two ways.

1. Make them feel guilty. Answer the phone with your best "I'm exhausted and have just been awakened from a deep sleep" voice. For anyone unsure how to perform this voice, it is a lot like the "I'm really sick, honestly" voice you used to fake when calling to skip work, except that you substitute a dash of hazy dreaminess for that note of feverish weakness.

2. Take caller revenge. Let the machine pick up. Then return their call the next morning, sometime well before 8 A.M.

FRIENDS AND FAMILY BOX
*When Is an Appropriate Time
to Call a New Parent?*

After their child graduates high school.

KEEPING OTHERS QUIET WHEN YOUR CHILD IS ASLEEP

Most parents know the simultaneous relief and anxiety that occurs when your child finally falls asleep. You are delighted to have some respite, but you are terrified lest some inopportune noise should waken your child. Few things are as grating to such a parent's ears as the loud, uncontrolled voice of a nonbaby person.

Probably the best way to encourage quiet in nonbaby people is to "enact" quiet yourself. If someone seems about to speak, go ahead and speak first in an elaborate stage whisper. It is best also to do an exaggerated cartoon tiptoe whenever you move, thus indicating to others that they should either remain still or do likewise.

Of course, subtle signs such as the above are more effective in an environment that is already relatively quiet. If your child falls asleep at a crowded restaurant, by contrast, you may have to engage in a maneuver such as "the Quarterback" (see figure 2).

Figure 2

DID YOU KNOW?
Your keys are in the refrigerator.

FRIENDS AND FAMILY BOX
Drunk or New Parent?

It can sometimes be difficult to tell whether a person is drunk or suffering from parental sleep-loss syndrome. One of the best ways to make that determination is to administer a field sleep-sobriety test.

Q: Can you count backward from ten?
Drunk (slurring slightly): "Ten, nine . . ."
New parent (imitating Transylvanian Count from Sesame Street with disturbing accuracy): "Ten, ha ha ha, nine . . ."

Q: Are you okay to drive?
Drunk: "Yes."
New parent: "Irrelevant. Can't find keys."

Q: Can you close your eyes, hold your arm out, and touch your finger to your nose?
Drunk: "Yes." (Closes eyes, puts finger in ear.)
New parent: "Are you serious? I could close my eyes, change a diaper, touch *your* nose, and then make coffee." (Closes eyes, falls directly asleep.)

THE LAST RESORT — DRUGGING YOUR CHILD

When all else fails, one of the most effective ways to get your child to sleep is to give them half a dose of nighttime cold medicine. It is possible that your spouse will not approve of giving the baby a drug that is not medically necessary. In this case, be sure to give your spouse a full dose of nighttime cold medicine before moving on to your baby.

5

What Goes In, Must Come Out

Peeing, Pooping, and Regurgitation Etiquette

PEES AND CUES
The Stain Game

The question: At a holiday party thrown by friends of the family, your daughter's diaper springs a leak and stains your acquaintances' Italian silk-covered couch. What should you do?

The answer: Although this is admittedly a dire situation, our patented **three-point stain-escape procedure** should help you to escape such inbroglios unscathed.

1. Disguise the evidence. Surreptitiously cover the stain with a pillow or, if available, the coat of another guest. This will not hide the stain forever, but it will buy you some time to collect your wits and remove your child from the immediate area.

2. Create "reasonable doubt." Urine stains are virtually indistinguishable from white wine stains—especially those of more full-bodied Chardonnays. Accordingly, parents of young children should always make sure to be holding a glass of white wine when visiting a private home. As soon as you detect a stain, drink off the remainder of the wine and set your empty glass somewhere close by. This will not necessarily clear your child of blame, but it will create confusion and plant a seed of reasonable doubt.

3. Frame another child for the offense. Once you have removed your own child, set a toy or similarly desirable object in the vicinity of the stain. Watch silently as an unsuspecting toddler is drawn into your trap. With luck, he will actually sit down and begin playing with the object, after which you can then watch *his* parents discover the stain and attempt their own version of the three-point escape procedure. (If the other parents do not immediately perceive the stain, you can direct them to it by whispering and pointing conspiratorially, implying that you know what their child did but are "cool" and not going to tell).

PEEING IN THE POOL

All children urinate in the pool, but it is nevertheless important for adults to maintain an illusion that this is not happening. In the case of older kids, the illusion is maintained by making them "go" before they get in the pool and by pretending the warm spots scattered throughout the pool are actually caused by the sun. In the case of infants, the clean-pool illusion is maintained by putting on a **swim diaper.**

Swim Diaper FAQs

DO "SWIM DIAPERS" REALLY WORK?

No. They do not work at all. They don't even come close to working. Anyone who has ever tried to put their child in a swim diaper *before* that ride to the pool or beach can attest to the fact that swim diapers leak like sieves even on dry land.

WHERE CAN I FIND A "SWIM DIAPER"?

Most stores have swim diapers placed conveniently in the diaper aisle next to the diapers that do work. You can easily differentiate the swim diapers because they are brightly colored—pink or blue or green—and significantly more expensive than regular, working diapers.

WILL OTHER PEOPLE KNOW THE "SWIM DIAPER" DOESN'T WORK?

Because of their bright colors and sleek appearance, the general public may be fooled into thinking that swim diapers have some sort of newfangled efficacy. Even parents of older children may assume that some new and effective swim-diaper technology has recently been developed. Parents of other infants will of course know that the diapers are bogus, but it is in their interest as much as yours to keep that fact hushed up.

IDENTIFYING THE "POOPETRATORS"

Urination etiquette is important, but when it comes to waste management, there is little doubt that the #1 issue for new parents is that dreaded #2. From discussion to diagnosis to the actual changing, soiled-diaper etiquette is an essential skill for any parent hoping to blend successfully with the rest of society.

Keeping Perspective

Because intestinal function is a key indicator of infant health, it is common for new parents to become morbidly intrigued by, perhaps even obsessed with, their child's bowel movements. They watch for them, chart them, and even exchange stories about particularly prodigious droppings. If you and your spouse find yourselves increasingly interested in your child's intestinal activity, you should try not to make your feelings public. Excitedly yelling, "Honey, you have to see this one," for example, is not appropriate unless you are changing a diaper in the privacy of your own home.

ETIQUETTE TIP

Most people do not find descriptions of your child's bowel movements, even particularly "epic" or unique ones, to be nearly as interesting as you do.

CHANGING DIAPERS

When it comes to diaper etiquette, there are three classic categories all parents should know: the **pungent diaper,** the **messy diaper,** and, perhaps most distressing to the uninitiated, the **exploding diaper.**

The Pungent Diaper

The essential thing when dealing with a pungent diaper is to avoid confined spaces. A foul-smelling nappy can make a crowded elevator ride seem endless (you should always take the stairs), while the same diaper on a walk in the park would generate little if any ill will.

One upside of the pungent diaper is that, if diagnosed quickly, it can give you the opportunity to **avoid changing the diaper yourself** by executing a quick pass to your partner.

PASSING THE POOP

The key to *passing the poop* is coming up with a plausible reason for handing off the baby. Obvious techniques include, "Could you hold her for a sec? I have to use the restroom," and "I just need to make a quick call," but these methods are too easily seen through. Any experienced spouse would execute a cautionary smell-check before accepting such a dubious handoff.

A more sophisticated handoff technique is that of **the seemingly kind offer.** If you say, for instance, "Would you like me to get you some cake?" your spouse is likely to be touched by the gesture and happily agree to hold the baby while you retrieve the promised dessert. By the time they sniff out your ruse, you will be long gone.

The Messy Diaper

There is one clear and absolute rule when preparing to change a messy diaper: *If you think that there cannot possibly be any more coming, there is more coming.* Parents changing slightly soiled diapers are usually diligent about having a "reserve" dia-per in hand should the baby begin a new round of defecation midchange. When changing a diaper that is already soiled almost beyond comprehension, however, these same parents tend to throw caution to the wind, reasoning that the child "couldn't possibly hold any more," or adopting a kind of Karmic, "How could it get any worse?" philosophy. This is pure naivete. Any veteran diaper-changer will tell you that **it can always get worse** and usually does.

The Exploding Diaper

The exploding diaper is every parent's etiquette nightmare—a diaper from which there is no shelter, no escape. It is a violent blast that erupts out the top of the diaper, blows out the sides of the diaper, or both. No matter where you are at the time—stuck in traffic, eating lunch at a company picnic, sightseeing atop the Empire State Building—the exploding diaper requires immedi-ate attention and an **emergency diaper change.**

THE EMERGENCY DIAPER CHANGE

While there are no hard-and-fast rules for emergency diaper changes, here are a few examples of what is acceptable and what is not.

Appropriate Places for an Emergency Diaper Change	Inappropriate Places
A picnic table	A picnic table where someone else is eating
The hood of your car	The hood of someone else's car

Appropriate Places for an Emergency Diaper Change	Inappropriate Places
The pool deck In the bathtub	The pool table In the bathtub when wife is attempting to take a soothing, candlelit soak after a brutal eight-hour day of baby care (see figure 1).

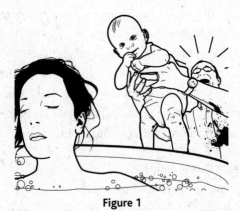

Figure 1

What Goes Down, Will Come Up: A Public Puking Primer

When preparing to deal with public regurgitation, it is first important to determine what weapons your child has in her arsenal. If you are able to predict what is coming, it will be considerably easier for you to mount an effective defense.

The "stealth" vomit. The stealth vomit is a particularly insidious form of regurgitation, executed so smoothly that you don't even know it's dripping down your shoulder or back. The best way to guard against a stealth attack is to check mirrors periodically or, if no mirrors are available, ask friends and/or passersby if you have any vomit on you.

Though clearly a liability when it comes to your own wardrobe, the stealth-vomiting child can be a formidable weapon when deployed against a more experienced baby "know-it-all." This is that person who, when your child is fussing, is sure that they know both the reason and the cure. If they diagnose "gas," for instance, they will probably want to demonstrate their patented "burping" technique. All you have to do is listen, learn, hand over the child, and watch them walk away with vomit dripping down their backside.

The "projectile" vomit. The problem with a projectile vomit is that the "cone of destruction" is not necessarily confined to you and the baby. Often it also encompasses friends, strangers, and/or the entire width of the produce aisle. If your child is a devotee of the projectile vomit, the thing that you should know from the start is that "burp cloths" simply will not cut it. You should be looking for some sort of "burp poncho."

The "drive-by" vomit. The drive-by vomit occurs when your baby vomits on a completely innocent bystander who had no idea what was coming. The obvious question in this case is, what do you say?

The first step is to **avoid any attempts at humor.** No matter how witty or self-deprecating the joke, it is a virtual guarantee that the regurgitation-covered victim **will not find it funny.**

The next step is to **offer to pay for the dry cleaning.**

And finally, if the offer is accepted, you should actually **hand over cash.**

The "Houdini." The Houdini is a regurgitation technique whereby the baby somehow pukes up more formula than she actually drank. One of the things new parents find themselves most surprised by is the sheer volume of vomit that their child is able to produce. The primary reason for their surprise is that the common euphemism "spitting up" suggests a mere thimbleful of saliva rather than a bellyful of partially digested formula. In order to prepare you for what actually lies ahead, we have created a more accurate list of regurgitation euphemisms.

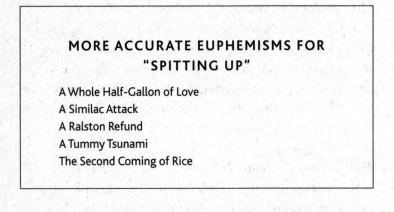

MORE ACCURATE EUPHEMISMS FOR "SPITTING UP"

A Whole Half-Gallon of Love
A Similac Attack
A Ralston Refund
A Tummy Tsunami
The Second Coming of Rice

6

Avoiding a Bad Wrap

Gift Etiquette

GETTING THE GIFTS YOU WANT
Registering

When it comes to baby showers, the first step in getting the gifts you want is to **register for them.** Many people are reluctant to do this simply because they are unsure of *where* to register and of *what* to register for.

Where: It is important to register at a place that is accessible to most of the people attending the shower. If the party is in Nebraska, for instance, don't bother registering at a Los Angeles boutique. It is also a good idea to register at a department store rather than at an all-baby store—that way you can exchange some of the baby stuff for a cappuccino maker, which you are definitely going to need once that baby is born.

What: If you register for cheap tacky things, you will receive cheap tacky things. If you register for expensive elegant things, you will still receive cheap tacky things, but at least people will feel bad about it.

Invitations and Announcements

Always send out classy shower invitations, birth announcements, and birthday party invitations. Because the niceness of baby gifts generally goes up in proportion to the cuteness of the baby, you should also make sure to include an extraordinarily adorable picture of your child in all birth announcements and birthday party invitations. If your child is unfortunate-looking, feel free to substitute a cute picture of someone else's child.

How to Encourage Gifts of Cash

Unlike weddings, baby showers rarely result in any significant fund-raising. There are, however, a few techniques you can use to encourage monetary giving.

Saying, "We have everything we need" while implying you in fact need a great deal more. When people ask you what you need prior to the baby shower, tell them you've already got everything you need in a voice that suggests you truly are needy but are too proud to ask for help. If they persist, say that just their presence at the shower will be a blessing to you and that is all you could ask for. If performed with the right mix of strength and vulnerability, this technique can go a long way toward producing a cash gift.

Setting up a "college fund" account. As the cost of collegiate education continues to skyrocket, more and more parents are setting up "college funds" for their infants and giving people an option to donate to that fund rather than purchase shower and birthday gifts. The useful thing about these funds is that they are really just bank accounts, and money can be removed at any time for "college-related expenses." A new big-screen television, for example, could be considered essential in keeping your child up-to-date with the kind of current cultural events—from world news to athletic achievements to cinematic expressions of the Zeitgeist—in which any good college would eventually expect them to be conversant.

Have a "themed" shower. "Themed" showers are all the rage these days, with concepts ranging from "Baby's Kitchen" (baby plates, spoons, bibs, bottles, high chairs) to "Midsummer Night's Dream" (crib, night-light, blankets, bedding, etc.). Those desiring cash gifts could go with a theme such as "Benjamin Franklin" or "Green and Crinkly."

DID YOU KNOW?
Books always make great shower gifts,
particularly ones that offer a humorous or
ironic look at the plight of new parents.

FRIENDS AND FAMILY BOX
What Not to Give at a Baby Shower and Why

A certificate that says, "Good for one night of free baby-sitting" and includes an expiration date: This is fine if you are a child, but if you are a grown-up, it is very lame.

Any outfit with a stain on it: Baby clothes are not "vintage," they are used.

Homemade stuff: Unless you're really good at making them, homemade things suck.

Anything you found on an amazing sale: When they return it they'll see how little you paid.

Anything bought on the black market: It is difficult to return.

Any toy that makes excruciatingly annoying noises: It is excruciatingly annoying.

Baby karaoke: Also excruciatingly annoying.

A Tiffany's sterling silver rattle: It's pretentious.

A loaded handgun: Obvious reasons.

Dropping Hints About Birthday and Holiday Gifts

One good way for new parents to ensure acceptable birthday and holiday gifts is to drop subtle hints as to what kinds of gifts would be appropriate.

Example: "Yes, her birthday is coming up . . . I don't know, anything, maybe some clothes . . . like there's a jumper in the J. Crew catalog, item number 487596-H, size 2t. That's the kind of thing that looks great on her. Number 487596-H, size

2t. And really, any of those colors would be great, as long as it's pink or yellow."

The Vicious Circle

Whenever gifts are opened at a shower or birthday party, it is traditional to form a kind of impromptu circle around which all gifts are passed upon opening. This gives the people who bought nice gifts a chance to bask in the congratulations of their peers and, perhaps more important, creates a feeling of shame in those who arrived with inadequate presents. Rest assured, no one who has endured the "vicious circle" ever brings a bad gift twice.

ETIQUETTE TIP
**There is no such thing as
a plastic "heirloom."**

What New Parents Say About Gifts vs. What They Actually Mean

Because no one ever says outright what they actually think of a gift, new parents sometimes find themselves confused about how to convey their feelings accurately. The following table will help both givers and receivers to communicate in gift-reception doublespeak.

WHAT A NEW PARENT SAYS	WHAT SHE ACTUALLY MEANS
You're so thoughtful.	*What were you thinking?*
This is so sweet.	*This is so cheap.*
Oh, you guys, this is way too expensive.	*This is perfect—you just moved up a notch on my Christmas card list.*
Oh my gosh, honey, you have to see this!	*I have no idea what this is supposed to be. Perhaps my spouse does.*
That's so great, we can totally use two of these.	*Regift!*

"Facing" the Facts

If you are unable to master the intricacies of gift-reception doublespeak, you should still be able to communicate your true feelings visually. The idea with visual communication is to say something noncommittal, like "Thank you so much," and then tilt the statement one way or the other through subtle shifts of facial expression.

THE GENUINE SMILE

To anyone paying attention, the genuine smile is a clear indication that you are happy with the gift. Be sure not to confuse the genuine smile with the *big fake smile*, in which the strain of forced insincerity is evident in a tightly knit brow or slight twitching of the eyes.

Fake Smile

THE UNENTHUSED HALF-SMILE WITH AIR HUG

The unenthused half-smile with air hug is the Ray Romano of gift responses. Amiable but unimpressive, it does a good job of saying, "Thanks for the moderate effort."

Unenthused Half-Smile

THE BEMUSED GRIMACE

The bemused grimace should be reserved primarily for gifts that are inappropriate or that you simply don't understand.

Bemused Grimace

GETTING RID OF GIFTS YOU DON'T WANT

Almost as important as getting the gifts you want is tactfully getting rid of the gifts you don't. This can be a touchy business, however, because when the gift-giver next comes to visit, they will most likely expect to see their gift in full effect. Unless you are willing to admit that you returned it, you may have to come up with a more creative strategy for getting rid of the gift while retaining evidence that it was not in fact returned.

Shrinkage

When it comes to dreadful clothing gifts, the best solution is shrinkage. Wash and dry the outfit on HOT several times until it shrinks beyond the point of wearability. Then, the next time the gift-giver visits, "attempt" to put on the outfit, demonstrate that it doesn't fit, and then lament how quickly children out-grow things. It will probably only take a shrunken sweater or two before they're giving you cash or gift certificates rather than trying to pick out garments themselves.

Sabotage

There was a time when new parents could "accidentally" drop an annoying toy and that would be the end of it. In today's world of seemingly indestructible synthetic toys, however, you may be forced to get a bit more creative in your methods of sabotage. Strategies you might consider include setting the toy down behind the rear wheel of your SUV, or smearing it in bacon grease and leaving it in the immediate vicinity of your dog. Remember, too, that although many synthetic toys are difficult to break, most of them will melt at high temperatures.

Regifting

Perhaps the most time-honored form of bad gift removal is regifting. The trick here is to wait until the gift-giver has seen the gift being used at your house, and then carefully rebox it, rewrap it, and present it as new at another child's party. You must of course avoid regiving the gift to the same people who originally gave it to you, and a good gift log (see below) can be quite useful in ensuring that this does not happen.

DID YOU KNOW

If you donate a gift to charity, even a tacky one that was originally bought on sale, you are allowed to deduct its full-market value from your taxes.

THANK-YOU CARDS

Few tasks are as odious to a new parent as the sending of thank-you cards, but it must be done if you hope to receive more gifts in the future. The first step in the process is to have someone you trust create a *gift log*—a booklet in which they write down what everybody gave so that you'll be able to send the appropriate thanks to the appropriate people.

The Gift-Log Scapegoat

You would of course love to simply send out a mass e-mail "thank-you" rather than handwriting dozens of cards. Unfortunately, this is blatantly inappropriate except in one instance, and that is if you are able to convince the keeper of the gift log to "take the fall" and become a *gift-log scapegoat* by somehow losing the log. Good scapegoats are people close to you who have already cultivated an aura of irresponsibility—flighty aunts, flaky little sisters, and chronically inebriated brother-in-laws can all make excellent scapegoats. Once they have "lost" the log, you can send out a mass e-mail saying how dismayed you are about this person's incompetence, and averring that although individualized cards are no longer possible, you'd still very much like to thank everyone for their gifts.

Writing the Thank-You Card

If you are unable to find a gift-log scapegoat, then you will have to go through with sending personalized, handwritten cards. Remember when writing that you should not only reference the gift, but you should also include at least a sentence on how that gift will make life so much better. Try also to use exclamation marks.

Example:

> Dear Elaine,
> Thank you so much for that homemade painting for the baby's room—I didn't even know you were an artist! It's amazing, because we were just saying last week how much we needed a pink and orange and lime-green watercolor to "challenge" the room's current décor. Now we have one!

7

The Hand That Rocks the Porta-Crib

Nanny/Baby-sitter Etiquette

HIRING CHILD CARE

Few infant issues are as fraught with etiquette-related anxi-
eties as hiring in-home child care. How do you choose the
right person? How much should you pay? Is that seemingly
benign baby-sitter about to turn your house into an after-hours
sin palace? In general, the best way to hire help is to **rely on
a recommendation from someone you trust.** If you are
unable to get a trustworthy recommendation, then you will
probably need to interview prospective sitters.

The "Obstacle Course" Interview

A common mistake made by new parents is asking interview
questions such as, "What is your child-rearing philosophy?" or
"How much experience do you have?" While these questions
may hold some mild academic interest, any knowledgeable

parent will tell you that what really matters when caring for a small child is **athleticism.**

Of course, it is one thing to know that reflexes and stamina are important and quite another to find ways of testing a potential baby-sitter's physical skills. It would not be appropriate to demand a fitness test or to throw things in the sitter's direction while saying, "Think fast." What you can do, however, is set up various physical challenges under the guise of conducting a "tour" of the house.

To test a baby-sitter's *toughness and agility,* for instance, you might rig an unbalanced vase to topple as you "accidentally" brush into it. Can she react in time to save your heirloom? Is she willing to dive for it? If so, she probably also has the skills to catch your little one as he begins to topple off the couch.

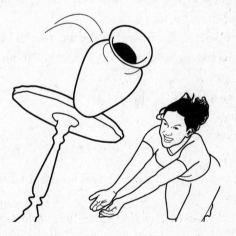

To test a sitter's *visual and cognitive acuity,* it is a good idea to leave something dangerous lying around—a sharpened meat cleaver, for instance—near the baby's bouncer. If she spots the offending object and either informs you or, even better, instinctually picks it up, you've got yourself a keeper.

Baby-sitter Types

Athleticism notwithstanding, it is also important to pick out the right personality type. Most potential baby-sitters will fall into one of the following four categories.

The Drama Girl

How to recognize: Generally attired in a scarf and/or beret, the drama girl will be constantly attached to a cell phone into which she repeats the phrase, "Oh my god, you're not going to believe this . . ."

The upside: As her name suggests, the drama girl will always have some kind of interesting story about why she is late.

The downside: She is always late.

The Cutie-Pie

How to recognize: Her outfit will invariably display a bare navel.

The upside: Gives husband something to look at/fantasize about.

The downside: Someone this attractive always has plans for Friday night. If she's agreeing to baby-sit, then the plans are at your house. Check those sheets before you go to bed!

The Overachiever

How to recognize: Brings four hours worth of homework and a large yearbook-layout project to a three-hour baby-sitting gig.

The upside: Has good grades and lots of after-school activities, which indicate initiative and responsibility.

The downside: With that many responsibilities, she won't have time to pay attention to your child. Also, you may be asked to write a saccharine "supporting letter" for her college applications essays.

The Loveable Loser

How to recognize: With frizzy hair and a slightly wrinkled skirt, the loveable loser usually carries a romance novel or copy of *Us* magazine.

The upside: Has nothing better to do on Friday and Saturday night.

The downside: Always asks you for fashion tips but never takes them. Style aside, however, loveable losers are perfect baby-sitting material.

D I D   Y O U   K N O W ?
Most baby-sitters believe that stolen food,
if taken in unnoticeable portions, does not
count against their day's calorie total.

THE NANNY LOOK

Hiring an occasional cutie-pie baby-sitter is one thing, but even the most confident new moms do not want a young, attractive woman flouncing daily around their house in low-rider jeans and a belly-baring top. Professional nannies know that their attractiveness level should be equal to or less than that of the mom they work for and, when necessary, will not hesitate to indicate their professionalism by undergoing a **nanny makeover.**

THE NANNY MAKEOVER

Wear oversized clothes: If you have a nice figure, wear oversized clothes in order to hide it. The clothes should be tidy and well-matched to give the appearance of competence, but they should not be sexy in any way.

Have bad hair: Never "do" your hair. If you are one of those women whose hair looks good even without being done, consider smearing a little baby food into it before leaving for your interview. This will make new moms feel comfortable and will also begin preparing you for the daily baby-food baths you'll be receiving if you do in fact get the job.

Look tired: One of the most difficult illusions to achieve is appearing as physically exhausted as a new mom. A little bit of pencil lead, spread judiciously, can give the appearance of some serious bags under the eyes.

Wear dreadful glasses: If you have attractive features, consider wearing some truly heinous glasses. A pair of coke-bottle lenses can disguise even the loveliest visage.

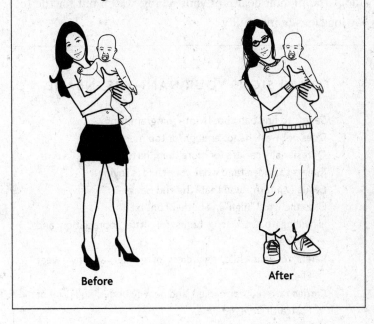

Before   **After**

How Much Should I Pay?

The rates for child care vary depending upon where you live, but in general they fall somewhere between $8 to $12 per hour (unless you are writing it off as a business expense, in which case $75 an hour is the norm). Some people believe in negotiating with sitters to get a lower price, but before doing that you might want to consider this question: Would you go with a heart surgeon just because he had the lowest rate? The best place to cut costs may not be on **the person caring for your child.**

Is Your Nanny Insane?

Unfortunately, not all nannies are sane. If you are concerned about the mental health of your nanny, watch out for the following signs of instability.

TOP 10 SIGNS YOUR NANNY IS INSANE

Seems to find baby books intriguing/amusing.

Does not wash hands enough, or too much.

Occasionally cackles for more than thirty seconds at a time.

Claims to understand what your child is saying.

Casually informs you that "the end is nigh."

Uses the word "nigh" in another context.

Is willing to work long hours for little appreciation and low pay.

Refers to your child, regardless of gender, as "my sweet Electra."

Carries tattered, earmarked, and heavily underlined copy of *Postcards from the Edge*.

Refers to Barney as "the Purple Prophet."

The "Nanny-Cam"

Once you have hired a baby-sitter or nanny, it is important to start looking for reasons to fire them. One interesting way to do this is to have a "nanny-cam" installed in your home. The theory behind nanny-cams is simple: Americans have a long, proud tradition of **watching things on television rather than actually doing them,** and nanny-cams allow you to apply this same principle to parenting. There are, however, some myths about nanny-cams that you should be aware of before getting one installed.

Myth: The nanny-cam allows you to ensure that nothing terrible is happening to your child.

Reality: It allows you to ensure that nothing terrible is happening to your child *on camera*. Devoted nanny-cam watchers often find themselves falling prey to the "horror movie" effect, where you are much more worried about what is happening offscreen than onscreen.

Myth: Nanny-cams are like having your own reality TV show.

Reality: Reality TV shows are heavily edited by entertainment professionals, and they still suck. You will find your nanny-cam footage sorely lacking in entertainment value, even if you do install the optional laugh track.

Myth: New technology allows you to connect to the Internet at work and receive live streaming video of what's happening in your home.

Reality: When was the last time new technology actually worked?

FIRING YOUR NANNY/BABY-SITTER

Letting people go is never an enjoyable task. Fortunately we live in an era of deferred responsibility, and there is really no reason that you have to fire your nanny or sitter directly. Instead, you can take a **passive-aggressive approach to termination.**

Passive-aggressive dismissals generally involve lying. Instead of saying, "I just don't feel comfortable with you in my home," for instance, you might say, "We're moving to Europe—but thank you so much for your help."

Another way to go is to establish an account from which you write your nanny a bad check or two. When she brings this to your attention, you can appear to be embarrassed and then, with a regretful look, claim that you don't have enough money to retain her services.

In the end, though, there is only one foolproof way to get rid of an incompetent child-care worker: Recommend her to someone else.

8

Playing Doctor

Medical Etiquette

THE PEDIATRICIAN

Visiting the pediatrician is always a nerve-wracking experience for new parents. In addition to dreading the inevitable shots, you desperately hope that your child checks out as healthy, normal, and "thriving." Sometimes it can seem that even those friendly weigh-ins are referendums on your parenting.

Giving Your Baby a Bottle Before the Weigh-in

A bit like cramming for a test, giving your baby a large bottle or breast-feeding immediately prior to his doctor's appointment will ensure that he is a good six to eight ounces heavier when he gets on that scale. This can easily make the difference between a sixty-eighth percentile weigh-in and an eightieth percentile weigh-in. If you're grading, that's the difference between a D and a B!

Note: The large bottle greatly increases the chances your baby will urinate prolifically when his diaper is removed prior to the weigh-in. Fortunately, it will most likely be the nurse-practitioner who is holding him at that time.

DAD'S CORNER
Being Ignored by the Pediatrician

Men visiting the pediatrician get a chance to experience, some for the first time in their lives, what it is like to be a woman buying a car. The pediatrician will inevitably address the mother when speaking, listen more attentively to the mother's questions, and smile reassuringly at the mother while giving you, at best, a look of mild disdain. If this isolation becomes too much for you to bear, there are several strategies you can employ to gain the attention of the pediatrician:

Nod excessively while the doctor is speaking.
Ask a lot of questions.
Wear an egregiously loud shirt.
Have a frank discussion with the doctor about your earnest desire to be included.
Feign hiccups or some other "involuntary" spasm.

Shots

The only thing new parents dread more than the weigh-in is THE SHOT. Few things are more distressing than holding your baby down while a stranger in a lab coat jabs a wicked-looking needle into her thigh. No one wants to be associated with the pain of that needle, so it is not uncommon for parents to engage in an unspoken, passive-aggressive game of "musical baby" in which the child is handed back and forth until the nurse-practitioner arrives with the shot. Whoever is holding her at that time loses. For those who don't like the randomness of this "Russian Roulette" approach, however, there are more devious options.

Playing dumb. If you have relatively good hearing, a good strategy is to stand close to the examination room door while blithely holding the baby. Act as though you don't know that the shot is on its way. Then, when you hear footsteps approaching, claim that you need to blow your nose and ask if your spouse can hold the baby "just for a second."

The restroom rescue. Go to the restroom, lock the door, and do not come out until you hear your child shrieking. Then rush into the room and "rescue" your child, picking her up and comforting her as the pain of the shot begins to subside.

Note: This "rescue" effect can be greatly enhanced by casting an accusing look at your spouse as you take the baby away.

Why Babies Cry So Much When They Get Shots

People often wonder why babies are so afraid of shots, not stopping to consider that what looks to them like a fairly small needle is utterly enormous relative to the baby. Imagine if you had to get a shot from a proportionately large needle.

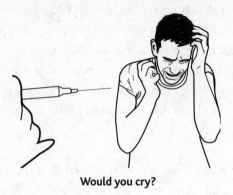

Would you cry?

Calling Your Pediatrician at Night

When it comes to phoning your pediatrician 1at night, always make sure to voice your question out loud *before* picking up the phone. "He's just not himself," "She seems to be swallowing weird," and "He looks a little orange" are all good examples of concerns that, if given a trial run, are unlikely to result in an actual phone call.

Calling Your Mom at Night

Of course, just because a question isn't dire enough to wake your pediatrician doesn't mean you shouldn't call someone—this is where your mom comes in. If you wonder why your mom seems so well trained at answering inane, repetitive, annoying questions at all hours of the day and night, simply wait until your own child turns three and you will understand completely.

HOME MEDICAL CARE
Giving the Baby Medicine

MANIPULATING YOUR CHILD

When it comes to administering medicine, many baby manuals advise that you try to trick your child into thinking it is a pleasant experience. This does not actually work.

Children are very perceptive and have long memories, and after the first time you put a nasty-tasting medication in their mouth under the guise of a fun culinary adventure, they're going to be on to you. You actually stand a much better chance of fooling your spouse.

MANIPULATING YOUR SPOUSE

Offer your spouse compliments such as, "You're so courageous," "You have such steady hands," and "You are so amazing with her. You can get that child to do anything!" Enhance the effect of these compliments by denigrating your own abilities, perhaps even offering some visual evidence of your incapacity, such as a bizarrely shaky hand or unpredictable elbow spasms. Then, when the time comes to administer the medicine, suggest that it would be kinder for the child to have the job done quickly and competently.

Taking the Baby's Rectal Temperature

See "Manipulating Your Spouse" above.

Making the Boo-Boo Better

Perhaps the most fundamental aspect of home medical care consists of making the boo-boo better.

Step One: The first step in making a boo-boo better is **pretending it wasn't particularly bad in the first place.** Parents who leap up in concern after a mild fall will inevitably create a sense of trauma in their child; parents who laugh and say "nice fall," on the other hand, may well escape the sobbing fit entirely.

Step Two: **Kiss the boo-boo.** The boo-boo-better kiss is a complex, highly technical procedure that requires both timing and accuracy.

Timing. Try to time the kiss for one of those brief rest periods between bouts of sobbing. Otherwise, it may get lost in the maelstrom.

Accuracy. It is essential that you kiss the actual area of the boo-boo. A kiss to the knee when an elbow boo-boo has occurred is quite likely to add "insult" sobbing to the original injury tears.

PREVENTIVE MEDICAL CARE

Wash Your Hands Before Touching the Baby

New parents are notorious for washing their hands. In fact, obsessive hand washing is one of the easiest ways to identify a new parent. There has recently been scholarly speculation that Lady Macbeth, heretofore thought to be childless, was in fact a new mother due to her meticulous hand hygiene.

Stay Away from the Pediatrician's Office

It is astonishing how many parents allow their child to run around in a doctor's office where *all the other kids are sick.* Many times a parent will take their child in for a sniffle and bring them home with the stomach flu. Remember, the worst place for a sick person is usually the doctor's office.

DID YOU KNOW?
Those toys in the pediatrician's office are actually I.Q. tests. Anyone who lets their child play with something previously handled by hundreds of sick kids is, according to the latest A.M.A. standards, just plain dopey.

Keep Strangers from Touching Your Child

One of the first things new parents are told is that they must keep random, unsterilized people from touching their newborn. This is not so difficult when you are at home, but when you are out in public, it can be quite a trial. Complete strangers will often feel compelled to touch a new baby. The fact that they are doing it out of kindness and not malice only makes it more difficult to turn them away, but you must be resolute. If you see a stranger approaching your child, any one of the following lines should help to slow their advance.

POLITE LINES TO KEEP STANGERS FROM TOUCHING YOUR CHILD

"Sorry, she's got a contagious rash."

"Have you taken steps to prepare for the apocalypse?"

"Careful, he bites."

"Freeze, scumbag."

"Can you spare some change?"

9

Sex After the Baby

Boudoir Etiquette

10

With Friends Like These

Peer Etiquette

WHO ARE THESE PEOPLE?

Every adult occasionally needs time with other grown-ups, but having a baby creates a whole new set of questions when it comes to peer interactions. Suddenly you have two very distinct categories of peers: New Friends (i.e., other people with babies, whom you're getting to know almost solely because they have babies) and Old Friends (people you used to hang out with and may like a great deal, but who do not have babies). Like matter and antimatter, it is rare and potentially dangerous for New Friends and Old Friends to interact, so this chapter is divided (much like your current friendship loyalties) into two separate sections.

MAKING NEW FRIENDS

All new parents need moral support from people undergoing similar trauma, and classes such as "Mommy and Me" provide a perfect opportunity to meet other new parents (usually moms). There are several categories of moms who tend to frequent baby classes, and once you learn to identify them, it will be much easier to sift through the pack and choose someone who meets your particular needs.

"Mommy and Me" Personality Types

The Know-It-All Mom: Know-it-all moms always have information at their fingertips, and they're not shy about sharing it. They know where music classes are offered and when the baby-swim hours start at the Y. They'll recommend a good pediatrician, a good toddler group, a good acupuncturist, you name it. Know-it-all moms are the same women who in high school always raised their hands and wound up with an A- for studious, competent, enthusiastic work that lacked inspiration and originality. These moms can be extremely useful friends if and when you get past the desire to slap their hand out of the air every time they raise it to make yet another "contribution" to group discussion.

The Yoga Mom: Yoga moms are a twenty-first-century reprise of the '70s flower-child mom. Big believers in New-Age philosophy, yoga moms are usually quite sweet and inclined to raise their children without the harsh constraints of discipline. Yoga moms can be very pleasant companions, provided you're not a Leo, because they've just never had good chemistry with Leos, unless *maybe* your rising sign is Pisces and then you could give it a try.

The Codependent Mom: Codependent moms are easy to recognize, because they will be talking to their infant as though the infant has some idea what they're saying. They will also be carrying an enormous bag containing every possible thing their child could want, and they will be clad, along with their child, in pseudomatching Laura Ashley outfits. Codependent moms are generally too engrossed with their child to have any time to make friends.

The Business Mom: Business moms are focused on "targeted nurturing" and can become disconsolate if their child is not similarly concerned with leveraging their quality time. At some point their cell phone will begin ringing with a call they "have to take." Business moms can be a bit intimidating at first but may be worth getting to know because they often have big houses with pools.

NEW FRIEND FAQ

Am I obligated to smile and make small talk with another new parent at the playground just because we both have kids?

Yes. You are taking your kids there to learn how to socialize with complete strangers, so it's only fair that you should learn, too.

The Internet Play-Date

Many twenty-first-century parents and children have become uncomfortable with the playground "scene," believing that it's a "total meat market" that is simply not conducive to meeting sensitive, nurturing playmates. This has led to the development of **Internet play-dating**—online services where your child can connect with like-minded babies by comparing lists of their likes, dislikes, and personal characteristics. The key to finding a good Internet play-date companion is, of course, crafting an attractive profile. Below is a sample play-dating profile, complete with helpful commentary in italics.

PLAY-DATE PROFILE

Personal characteristics:
I am: a baby
Seeking: another baby
Height: 2′ 6″
Weight: 19 pounds
Hair: Not yet
Smoking: No

The last three books I read were:
Goodnight Moon
Pat the Bunny
The collected poetry of Pablo Neruda—*It is important to include at least one book that makes you look artistic and sensitive.*

My most humbling experience:
Let's face it—any time you crap yourself it's a humbling experience.

The five items I can't live without:
My yellow blanket
My green blanket
My pink blanket
My mom—*It is always good to have at least one heartstring-tugging element in your list.*
My mom's boobs—*There's nothing wrong with taking the question literally.*

Fill in the blanks:
La La **is sexy.**
Tinky Winky **is sexier.**

In my crib, you'll find:
Cheap toys, some urine stains, and a lot of stuffed animals, but not me—I learned to jump out yesterday and land on my head!

What I enjoy:
Moonlight crawls, bottles by candlelight, and the music of David Gray—*No one actually listens to David Gray, but for some reason it's cool to say you do.*

Why you should get to know me:
I'm sensitive, curious, healthy, energetic, honest, know how to get what I want, have a great smile, am not afraid to cry, and can pee almost six feet in the air.

Conducting the Play-Date

COMPARING YOUR CHILDREN

Once you have found a suitable parent-baby combination and have begun your play-date, it is time to set about the task of **covertly comparing your children.** The idea is to make awkward conversation about innocuous baby issues—how is she sleeping, what foods is she eating, etc.—while closely observing one another's children in an attempt to answer the truly pertinent questions: Is their child as cute as your child? Are they walking already? Talking? How's their vocabulary?

One way to glean this information tactfully is to underrate your own child's achievements. You might say, for example, "I'm a little worried about Lilly's vocabulary. She only says 'mama' and 'dada' and a few other words." This faux admission should encourage the other mom to open up about her own child's speaking skills. Remember that your goal here is not to compete with the other mom overtly, but rather to reassure yourself and your spouse that you do indeed have the more impressive child.

FORCING YOUR CHILDREN TO INTERACT

At some point during the play-date it is customary to force your children to interact while simultaneously exclaiming, "Oh my God, that's so cute." Encourage your child to hug and/or kiss the other child while you take a picture. The fact that your child is excruciatingly uncomfortable is irrelevant. The cuteness of the picture will, in the long run, more than make up for this emotional trauma.

How to End a Play-Date

Many toddler play-dates end in the same way—with a fight over a toy. As the fight begins, each parent should look at the other apologetically and say to their child, "Honey, can you share the toy? Sweetheart . . . Honey, can you share?" Your children will of course ignore you completely. As the battle between the toddlers escalates into shrieking and pulling, one or the other parent will seize the toy in a kind of Solomonic gesture, after which both children will sob reproachfully for the remainder of the play-date.

OLD FRIENDS

When it comes to your old friends, you will probably notice a distinction in the first few months between the *baby people* and the *nonbaby people*. The baby people may have been among your least "cool" friends before the birth, but now they are definitely the place where you will want to put your limited friendship energy. If you are having a hard time discerning between the baby people and the nonbaby people, the following information should help you decide.

Baby People vs. Nonbaby People

What they said when you told them your wife was pregnant:

Baby people: Congratulations!
Nonbaby people: Is it yours?

What they brought to dinner when you were pregnant:

Baby people: Dessert
Nonbaby people: A bottle of wine

What they brought to the hospital after you gave birth:

Baby people: Flowers and/or "Congratulations" balloons
Nonbaby people: Yeah, right

When the baby starts crying, they say:

Baby people: Oh, come here, sweetheart, it's okay.
Nonbaby people: (Looking at watch) Do you know how long
this is going to go on?

When you ask them to hold the baby for a minute:

Baby people: Cradle the baby comfortably in one arm
Nonbaby people: Utilize the two-handed "straight-arm"
method

The "Straight-Arm" Method

Using the Baby to Avoid "Old Friends" You Never Really Liked in the First Place

One of the best things about having a child is that it creates a built-in excuse for discontinuing irksome acquaintances. If people you don't particularly care for invite you to a dinner party, for instance, you can now claim that you couldn't get a sitter. If they call and want to stop by, you can claim that the baby is sick. Whatever attempt these pseudofriends make to reestablish connection with you, your baby has the power to foil it.

Convincing Old Friends to Have Babies So That You Won't Be Desperately Alone

Unfortunately, your baby also has the ability to foil connections with people you actually like. Caring for a young child can be very lonely, and thus you may wish to **convince your old friends to have children so you won't be desperately alone.** If you are unsure how to go about this, think about the lies your "friends" with children told you when you were considering getting pregnant. Morning sickness "only lasts a couple of weeks." Labor is "a beautiful experience." Breastfeeding makes you feel "really natural, really connected to what's important." And, of course, "You'd be surprised how little sleep a person actually needs."

POSTBABY PHONE ETIQUETTE TIPS

Because many of your old friends no longer live in the same place as you, it is important to practice good baby phone etiquette if you want them to keep taking your calls.

HAVE AT LEAST ONE ADULT VOICE ON THE ANSWERING MACHINE

It can occasionally be cute when a machine says something like, "Hi, we're not here right now, but leave a message for Ted, Anne, or Zoe after the beep," and then there's the sound of a baby in the background going "ohhhhh."

It is another thing entirely for a someone to call and hear, "Hi wewa dohom rhinows messa da hemsess mama BEEEP."

DON'T USE SPEAKERPHONE

It is of course nice to have a hands-free option when you're caring for the child, but imagine the plight of your interlocutor. The various shrieks, bangs, burps, and giggles suggest that perhaps you are not giving full attention to the conversation.

LOCK YOUR CELL PHONE

Babies are obsessed with cell phones. No one has yet discovered exactly why this is, but researchers suspect that it has something to do with the capacity to bedevil people not in their immediate vicinity.

The problem with letting your baby hold your cell phone is that when they press the speed dial, and they will, it is going to call one of your friends and leave several minutes of "gooing" and rustling on their answering service. This "prank" calling can severely hamper your ability to get in touch with your friends: People whose names begin with *A* rarely even pick up the phone when caller ID shows a new parent's phone number, reasoning that it is merely the child calling again.

FRIENDS AND FAMILY BOX:
What to Say When Your Friend Puts the Baby on the Phone

"Hi Emma! How are you doing?"
[No response]
"Are you having a good day today?"
[No response]
"Bet you're getting pretty big, huh?"
[Muffled slurping sound—could be gas]
"Well, I can't wait to see you!"
[Banging sound]
"Could you put your mama back on the phone?"
[Long uncomfortable silence until mom finally takes phone back]

AVOIDING TODDLER-SPEAK

As entertaining as toddlers and their linguistic foibles can be, it is important for new parents to remember when they are out with old friends that it is not entirely cool to talk like their baby.

When nature calls, for example, make sure to ask, "Where is your restroom?" instead of "Where's the potty?"

When out with other adults, refer to your spouse by their actual name instead of "Daddy" or "Mama" (an exception to this rule is if you are middle-aged, from the Midwest, and have

three or more children, in which case the whole "Daddy"—
"Mama" thing can be kind of sweet).

When a waiter tells you the restaurant is out of the duck,
calmly order chicken or fish rather than bursting into tears and
sobbing, "I . . . want . . . my . . . duuuuuck!"

ETIQUETTE TIP

Try to remember that the edginess of baby music is
relative, and your nonbaby friends may not appreciate
Hi-5's latest CD even though they do in fact rock
compared to The Wiggles.

TEACHING YOUR DAUGHTER TO FLIRT

Your male friends may claim not to like babies, but most men's
convictions go straight out the window when they think a cute
girl likes them—even if that girl is only fourteen months old.
The female's approval makes them feel elevated, superior to
other men who are not the recipients of such eye-batting and
smiles. If your daughter can master phrases such as "so big"
and "so strong," your friend may become so entranced by his
miniature admirer he won't even realize he's been co-opted
into a series of pretend tea parties.

TEACHING YOUR SON TO LIE ABOUT LOVE

Perhaps the best way to ensure that your female friends remain baby friendly is to encourage your son to say "I love you" long before he actually has any idea what those words mean. The female in question will inevitably be touched by this bogus pronouncement and will henceforth be more likely to accept your son's misbehavior and accede to his every request. It won't take your son long to grasp a connection between the words leaving his mouth and the behavior of the women who hear them. You will thus not only have cemented your postbaby friendships, but will also have prepared your son for the essential task of lying about love later in life to get what he wants from women.

11

Labor Pains
Workplace Etiquette

WORKING "WHINE TO FIVE"

Many people assume that babies are a hindrance to achieving career success, but this is not necessarily the case. If exploited judiciously, young children can provide solid excuses for tardiness and incompetence, create opportunities for "schmoozing" child-friendly supervisors, and even serve as a heartstring-tugging trump card when it comes time to pass out those pink slips. The trick is to leverage the child to your benefit while avoiding the etiquette pitfalls that so often hinder parentally challenged employees.

PARENTHOOD PITFALLS
Discussing Your Child with Colleagues

There is nothing wrong with discussing your baby with coworkers during coffee or lunch breaks, particularly when one or more of them has also recently had a child. If you are concerned that your interlocutor might be bored with the discussion, however, it is good baby etiquette to look for signs of *conversation fatigue* such as yawning, stretching, reading a magazine or, in the case of a male colleague, attempting to "hang" himself with his tie.

FRIENDS AND COWORKERS BOX
Getting Out of a Conversation with a New Parent

If you find yourself caught in a baby-related conversation with one or more of your parentally challenged coworkers, there are several techniques you can use to extricate yourself with tact.

Pretend you need to use the restroom. This time-honored conversation-avoidance technique is usually quite effective. The only problem is that if the new parent follows you into the restroom to continue the conversation, you are essentially trapped for the duration of your visit.

Pretend you have work to do. You are, after all, at work, so it is not beyond the realm of possibility that you might actually have work that needs to be done.

Be polite but honest. Say, "I'm sorry, but this is not a conversation I can bear any longer. I'm going to go elsewhere. Have a nice day!"

Feign illness. New parents are notoriously paranoid about transporting germs home to their baby, and a single vehement sneeze in their direction will most likely end the conversation and send them scurrying for cover.

Pictures in Your Cubicle

New parents always want baby pictures in their cubicle, but how many is too many? Let's put it this way. If your coworker has a picture of J. Lo in his cubicle, you assume he's a fan. If he has two pictures, you assume he is a really big fan. But if he has more than a dozen? It is best not to give the impression that you're stalking your own child.

The Humming/Singing of Baby Songs

The humming and/or singing of baby songs is inappropriate in any adult situation, but this is particularly true at work where people have to be around you the entire day. Baby songs are extraordinarily, insidiously catchy, and the contagion can spread very quickly. The last thing your company needs is an office full of people humming "Itsy Bitsy Spider" or singing the theme to Sesame Street.

When you are in the company of others and find yourself possessed by a particularly infectious melody, it is imperative that you **do whatever is necessary to stop singing.** If while using the lavatory you find yourself singing the "Yes, I'm goin' to my potty potty" song, you might try bashing your head against the side of the toilet (figure 1).

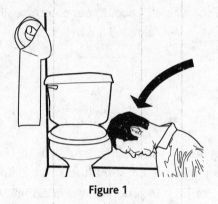

Figure 1

If this does not stop the singing, try putting your head between the stall and the stall door and allowing a coworker to slam the door with vigor (figure 2). Whatever it takes, **you must stop singing that damnable song.**

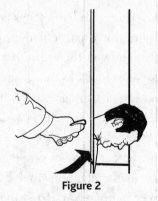

Figure 2

Conducting Meetings While Half-Asleep

Occasionally, you will awaken in a meeting and realize that people are expecting you to respond to a question. Simply nod enthusiastically and say, "Yes!" A positive attitude can go a long way in today's corporate America, even if it has little to do with the matter at hand.

Using the Fact That You Both Have Children to Curry Favor with Your Boss

If your boss or immediate supervisor has recently had a child, you should see this as a clear and present opportunity to curry favor. There is a good chance that your boss is as desperate as you for some kind of solace, and you may be surprised to find that bosses who would not even have considered hanging out with a lowly junior employee before becoming parents are **now pursuing you** in search of a reliable play-date partner. You may not be much of an employee, but setting yourself up as a trusted child-care partner could go a long way toward upping that year-end bonus.

USING YOUR CHILD AS AN EXCUSE FOR TARDINESS AT WORK

When using your child as an excuse for tardiness and/or incompetence, you have a variety of options.

The Gross-out Excuse "She vomited all over me just as I was leaving. I had to change my outfit, and I think I've still got some in my hair."

Why it works: If the description is vivid enough, your supervisor will be far too busy trying to control their own gag reflex to worry about disciplining you.

The Sympathy Excuse "Sorry, I had to take her to the doctor's. I'm really worried about her!"

Why it works: It is very un-PC to dock someone's pay because they have a sick child.

The Novelistic Excuse "She wobbled down the spiral stairs, her alabaster skin a blithe contrast to the dark cloud of need in her eyes. 'Mommy no go,' she crooned in a hymn of timeless longing, a paean to the bond between mother and daughter, an almost atavistic murmur that told me I'd be just a little bit late."

Why it works: In the time it takes you to reach the end of the explanation, your supervisor will have forgotten what they asked.

The Blame-Shift with Self-Promotion Kicker "Sorry, the nanny was late. I had words with her, and let's just say it won't happen again."

Why it works: Blame-shifting displays your bureaucratic savoir faire, and your discipline of the child-care worker makes you appear managerial and in charge rather than discombobulated and late.

PROCRASTINATION

Procrastination is a time-honored labor practice, but having a baby at home can help you take your workplace procrastination techniques to a whole new level.

Baby-related procrastination options
  Online baby stores
  Live-streaming nanny-cam
  Live-streaming breast milk
  Staring blankly at baby pictures, feeling guilty you're not at home
  Washing vomit off shirt
  "Kegel" exercises

Using Your Child to Avoid Getting Fired

Depending on the temperament of your boss, having an infant in your corner could be a real job saver during economically turbulent times. The image of you with a helpless, dependent child can be a powerful firing deterrent to any but the most coldhearted supervisor. During a holiday party or work-related social retreat, try to get a picture of you, your boss, and your child. If at all possible, talk your boss into actually holding the child while the picture is snapped. Then, when you feel that a round of company belt-tightening is impending, send your boss the picture signed with a faux note from your little one. It should read something to the effect of, "Dear Mr. Smith, thank you so much for helping my daddy provide for our family. I say a prayer for you every night. Big hugs and kisses, Amanda."

12

You Bite It, You Buy It

Shopping Etiquette

THE SUPERMARKET
Putting the Cart Before Remorse

When shopping with young infants, it is best to keep them in a "Baby Bjorn" on your chest. For toddlers and babies too big for the Bjorn, however, there are a variety of shopping-cart options to consider: **miniature "shopper-in-training" carts, the cargo area of the cart, the undercarriage of the cart,** and, of course, **the traditional baby-seat area of the cart.**

Shopper-in-training carts, while they do look cute, are too low to the ground for other shoppers to see and are thus a magnet for accidents. They also tend to give your toddler a false sense of efficacy: Why shouldn't they get what they want, they reason, when they're driving the cart? The fact that they're driving it into walls, shelves, and other shoppers does not lessen their sense of entitlement. Shopper-in-training carts are more commonly known by their informal name, "Lawsuit-waiting-to-happen carts."

The cargo area of the cart is always attractive to children, because it gives them the feeling of being chauffeured. And not unlike teenagers in their first chauffeured limo, they will occasionally feel compelled to throw things out at innocent passersby. Note: For everyone's sake, do not pick up eggs until right before you check out.

The undercarriage of the cart is where children most want to be, because it is both dirty and dangerous. Children stowed away in the cart undercarriage are mere millimeters away from getting run over and are sure to come away with a generation's worth of accumulated grime on their hands and clothes. The good news, however, is that they can cause less collateral damage once they have given up the high ground.

The baby cart seat is a time-honored shopping tradition and keeps the baby directly in front of you with no access to the cargo area of the cart. The only real downside of this position is that it gives the child ample elevation to grab items—fruit, in particular — off the shelf and bite into them before you realize what is happening.

When Your Child Creates a Display-Item Avalanche

The practice of infant shelf grabbing generally climaxes with a **display-item avalanche,** in which a carefully constructed pyramid of products is toppled by your child's well-timed grab from its base. There is a two-part strategy for dealing with such in-store calamities: **distraction and diversion.**

The **distraction** here is simple to accomplish, because the

THE "YOU BITE IT, YOU BUY IT" RULE

There is a crucial difference between gumming a piece of fruit and actually biting it—i.e., breaking the skin. If the fruit has merely been gummed, it is permissible to wipe it on your sleeve and put it back on the shelf. The worst that will happen is that some innocent shopper will catch your baby's cold and suffer for the next week or two.

If there are actual teeth marks in the fruit, however, you should probably just go ahead and buy it. If you are poor and cannot afford to buy the masticated fruit, your best bet is to place it somewhere completely random—behind a few boxes of tampax, for instance—when no one is looking. By the time someone discovers the rotting remnants, you will be long gone.

avalanche itself has already provided it. In an aisle avalanche, as in a freeway accident, there is generally a good deal of "looky-loo" traffic (see figure 1). Take advantage of this traffic

Figure 1

to create your **diversion:** Remove the avalanche-causing product from your child's hand and give it to the child of another distracted parent (figure 2), thus deflecting culpability from your own child.

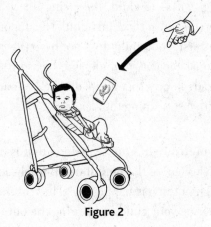

Figure 2

The "Getaway" Cart

If your child refuses to relinquish the telltale product, there is a daring "last resort" option you may want to consider. Physically remove the child from your cart and put him into the cart of a distracted stranger. By the time the supermarket manager calls you to claim your lost child, the avalanche furor will have passed and you may actually have had the opportunity to finish your shopping in peace.

The In-Store Meltdown

In the days when spankings were permissible, parents had a legitimate weapon with which to combat their child's guerilla meltdown tactics of crying, kicking, screaming, and throwing.

In today's world, however, you will need to go with a kinder, gentler meltdown-containment technique.

"Reason" with your child. Some parents use the technique of "reasoning" with the child, theorizing that if you treat her like an adult she will act like an adult. This theory is faulty for two reasons: First, your child does not have the language skills or the emotional capacity to understand reason; second, everyone else already knows that and will think you are an idiot for reasoning with a screaming toddler.

Ignore the meltdown. One technique that is currently popular is simply to ignore the meltdown. Blithely continue shopping as though nothing is happening. The real trick here is not so much ignoring your child as ignoring the outraged stares of other shoppers appalled at your lack of compassion for a child so obviously in need.

Threaten to leave the store. One increasingly popular technique is threatening to leave the store. The only problem with this method is that it is wholly ineffective. Your child does not mind if you leave the store; in fact, they want you to leave, so this threat provides them with little incentive to calm down. If you do make the threat and are then forced to back it up, the polite thing to do is **leave a small tip on your cart** for the poor grocery bagger who will have to return all your unbought goods to the shelf.

Have your own meltdown. A too-often overlooked technique for containing a toddler meltdown is staging your own even more impressive meltdown. This "shock and awe" approach is designed to stun your child into confused silence. Go ahead and cry, shriek, even throw something from the cart if you have to—after all, what do you have to lose, your dignity?

DID YOU KNOW?
Although it is illegal to abandon your child, there is no law against bluffing.

The Checkout

There is a kind of unwritten competition between new parents to see who can delay the checkout line the longest. If you find that you are not quite as successful in this contest as some of your peers, here are a few tips for achieving checkout-delay success:

Advanced parental checkout delay techniques

Ask cashier to void random items that baby has placed on the conveyor and have already been rung up.

Dispute the price of some insignificant item so that the cashier calls for a "price check."

Ask child to relinquish item she is holding so that it can be scanned. Rather than taking item from her when she refuses, attempt to persuade her verbally.

Argue that a long-expired coupon should still be valid.

Exclaim, "Oh my gosh, I forgot diapers!" and run to retrieve them.

Do not pay for groceries in cash.

Attempt to comfort child as you rummage for your check-book and write out the check. Cross out your mistake and void the first check. Take your time on the second one to make sure you get it right. Now that you've got it, go ahead and balance that book before handing over the check.

THE MALL
Getting Through Doors with a Stroller

Many strip mall and department stores are not equipped with either electronic door openers or attentive gentlemen, so you may have to get the stroller through the doors on your own. The question is not so much how to get the door open as how to get all the way through it **without spilling your Starbuck's coffee.** The three most popular entry techniques are *the one-hander, the butt-out,* and *the cup-holder caper.*

The one-hander. The idea with the one-hander is to enter sideways, pushing the door open with the cup-holding hand and then pulling the stroller through with your other hand. One benefit to this technique is that when your coffee spills, it will be nowhere in the vicinity of the baby and will scald only your hand.

The butt-out. The butt-out is an advanced door-entry technique that involves keeping both hands on the stroller while backing through the door in a "piked" position. This move has a high degree of difficulty, and there is some chance that when your coffee spills, it will splash down onto the baby.

The cup-holder caper. The key to the cup-holder caper is putting your coffee into one of those cheap add-on plastic cup holders that attaches dubiously to the frame of the stroller. Once you have placed the coffee into it, the cup holder will almost immediately invert, dumping your entire cup of coffee onto the ground and freeing you to enter the doors without further anxiety about spillage.

Finding an Elevator When You've Got a Stroller

The trick to finding an elevator at the mall is to think of the least convenient place it could be. In other words, try to think with total illogic. Would it make sense to put an elevator near the stairwell or near a major entrance or exit? Then it will be as far away from those places as possible. Would it make sense to have the elevator easily recognizable and accessible for handicapped people and parents with small children? Then look around corners, behind arches, anywhere that is almost completely hidden from view.

Bribing Your Child

Perhaps the most universal infant shopping technique is simple bribery: "If you let Mommy try on three sweaters, we'll go and buy you a toy." Some parents will attempt to offer clothing or book bribes, but these efforts are usually quite transparent and any competent infant will reject them out of hand. A far more effective bribery technique is the *extravagant offer with backdoor caveat*.

The key to making an extravagant offer with backdoor caveat is to emphasize the initial offering rather than the fine-print qualification: "If you can hold still for ten minutes, we're going to PICK OUT ANY TOY YOU WANT that we both approve of." The children are usually so hypnotized by the initial possibility that they accept the qualification without really thinking about it.

Engaging in Stale, Obligatory Banter with a Well-Meaning Salesperson

Whether you are at the supermarket or the mall, it is inevitable that either a salesperson or another customer will offer some well-intentioned, child-related platitude to which you feel obligated to respond. There is no rule, however, that says you can't make these obligatory responses a little more interesting.

"Changes your life, doesn't it?"
Usual response: "It sure does," followed by a fake smile.
More interesting response: "Actually, not at all," followed by an ironic grimace.

"Greatest time of your life."
Usual response: "It sure is," followed by an inauthentic smile.
More interesting response: "Well, maybe not as great as that drug-and-sex filled jaunt to Cabo during spring break junior year, but it's pretty great."

"What a gift!"
Usual response: "It sure is," followed by a faux smile and a brief head-rub of child.
More interesting response: "I would have settled for a bottle of Jack and some concert tickets."

13

The Baby Wears Prada

Beauty Etiquette

BABY CLOTHES
What Baby Sizes Actually Mean

Most new parents have no idea what baby sizes actually mean. If your child is nine months old but has a large head, for example, would they wear a twelve-to-eighteen-month hat? The following should give you an idea of what baby sizes actually translate to in real life.

BABY SIZE	WHAT IT MEANS
Three to six months	too small
Six to twelve months	wash it once; now too small
Twelve to eighteen months	sold out
2T	one size fits all

Designer Baby T-Shirts

One of the most popular recent trends in baby clothes is tiny T-shirts with the name of a famous designer printed on them: Versace Baby, Calvin Klein Baby, and, perhaps most redundantly, bebe Baby are all good examples of this trend. Parents who want to send the same message without paying the 400 percent markup for a designer T-shirt can buy a normal baby shirt and then have one of the following messages printed on it.

"Pretentious Baby"
"My parents have taste. No, really, seriously, they do."
"My parents have way too much money and all I got was this lousy T-shirt."

Infant Baby Shoes

Because newborn infants cannot walk or even crawl, tiny infant baby shoes are probably the single most superfluous item in the history of the clothing industry, outdistancing even the calf-warmers worn by women in the early to mid '80s. That said, however, Baby Jordan basketball shoes are pretty darn cute.

BABY BOY HAIRSTYLES

The "California" Too-Much-Hair-Gel Look: Since the late '90s, twenty- and thirty-something men have been cutting their hair short and then mussing it up with way too much hair gel. This style has recently also begun to catch on with little

DO YOUR BABY'S STAINS MATCH?

One of the most delicate issues of infant fashion etiquette is the matching of stains. Many people have no idea, for instance, whether an orange-juice stain goes well with a messy smear of chocolate (it does) or whether a dash of cherry popsicle would be just the thing to tie together splotches of split pea and sweet potato on the baby's sky-blue jumper (no).

The most important thing when matching your stains is to *stay within the same color family*. Grape juice, for instance, is a warm, earthy-colored stain. It goes nicely with dirt, mashed peas, and smeared squash, so you might want to plan a grape-juice-stained baby's activity accordingly. A fading watermelon stain, on the other hand, should probably be complemented by other pastels: a splash of apple juice, a dab of mint ice cream, or a deluge of regurgitated formula could all do a good job of bringing that watermelon stain to life.

boys and can be a very cute look—especially when accompanied by bleached teeth and a too-tight black T-shirt.

The Baby Mullet: The baby mullet can be an adorable hairstyle on a small boy, as long as you make sure that it isn't too long. Think Sting mullet as opposed to Billy Ray Cyrus mullet. And, of course, lose the mullet before your son hits puberty.

Gangsta Baby: The popularity of hip-hop fashion has filtered down to the under-two set, and hairstyles are no exception. The nice thing is that many baby boys need not shave their heads since they are already bald, and all that needs to be added is a black do-rag and clothes baggy enough that they could conceivably hold a concealed pacifier.

Is Your Little Girl Bald?

Few things are as traumatic for parents of a little girl as prolonged baldness: It is one thing to be hairless at three weeks, and quite another when the baldness persists past the first twelve months. Yet this is the case with almost 50 percent of little girls. Fortunately, modern style has melded with modern technology to provide a variety of options.

Hats: If you are fortunate enough to live in a cold climate, you can go with a cute winter cap virtually all day long. If you live in a warm climate, you'll have to go with a brimmed hat and say that its purpose is to keep off the sun (you might suggest that even indoors those reflected rays could do some damage).

Bows: The idea with bows is to clip them to whatever hair there is. If there is not even enough hair to clip to, then you should avoid using a bow—those elastic headband bows bespeak real desperation.

Spray-on hair: The same spray-on technology used by desperate, balding men can also be used by the desperate parents of a still-bald baby. Unfortunately, it's no more effective on the baby than it is on the men.

Wear pink: The main thing when battling baldness is for a little girl to wear pink or, even more to the point, a T-shirt that says, "I'm not a boy."

Ways to Subtly Blame Your Spouse for Features You Dislike in Your Child

Blame it on parents-in-law: He's got your dad's [insert undesirable feature here].

Feign wonderment: I wonder where those ears came from?

Offer a backhanded compliment: It's good that she got your nose. I mean, that's a powerful nose. That's a nose that means business.

FRIENDS AND FAMILY BOX

What to Say If Your Friend's Baby Is Ugly

"Oooh, look at the baby!"
"Oh, baby."
"He's getting so big!"
"She's really something."
"Look at the hands/feet on him!"

Should You Buy One of Those Baby Gap Boating Hats for Your Son Just Because All the Other Yuppie Parents Are Buying Them for Their Sons?

Yes.

Ear Piercing

Piercing is of course a personal choice. In general, though, it is never too early to start modifying your daughter's body to increase her fashionability. Other potential modifications include: the baby nose pierce, baby hair extensions, baby high heels, and, of course, the baby lower-back tattoo.

FASHION DON'TS

It is fine for parents to have fun dressing their children, and certainly there are a lot of interesting choices out there. Please be sure, however, to avoid the following fashion faux pas.

DON'T	BECAUSE
Put makeup of any kind on your infant daughter.	People who do this are suffering from a damaging psychological condition known as Calvin Klein syndrome by proxy.
Put your son in one of those baby tuxedos.	While not quite as bad as dog tuxedos, they're still really bad.
Buy your daughter baby Uggs.	No person, child or adult, has ever not looked stupid in Uggs.
Dress your daughter in one of those Porn * T-shirts.	One hopes the reasons are obvious.

Don't	Because
Dress your son in one of those Porn * T-shirts.	Equally obvious reasons.
Buy your daughter miniskirts or low-rise jeans.	The diaper ruins the look.
Dress your baby in black	Coffee, cigarettes, and berets are all bad for babies.

Is Your Child as Cute as Other Kids?

Parents may be aware that they are blinded by love and may find themselves curious to know how, in an impartial universe, their child's cuteness actually rates against the cuteness of other children.

If you are concerned that your child may not be as cute as other children, watch out for the following clues:

You and/or your spouse are yourselves unfortunate-looking.

You find yourself using conditional phrases when discussing your child's looks—"When she gets hair," "When she smiles," "If the rest of his head catches up to his ears."

You've ever uttered the words "awkward period."

Other people's first comments about your child generally involve size, hair color, or personality. Be particularly wary of the phrase, "What a character!"

Parents Dressing Like Their Children

The reason babies look cute in pink T-shirts and green stretch pants is that babies *are* cute. In anything. They are babies. Women who dress like their babies are not actually babies and often do not look cute in pink T-shirts and green stretch pants.

14

The Party Pooper

Event Etiquette

PARTIES
Should You Bring the Baby?

From birthday and anniversary parties to dinners and backyard barbecues, there are a variety of social functions to which it may or may not be appropriate to bring the baby. If the invitation says "black tie," "adults only," or "no tantrums, please," it is probably not appropriate to bring your child; if, on the other hand, it is addressed to "the Wilson family" and has teddy bears stenciled on the card, you can rest assured that your little one will be welcome. Failing any such obvious signs, your best bet is simply to **ask whether or not it is okay to bring the baby.**

FRIENDS AND FAMILY BOX

Possible Responses When a Friend Asks if It's Okay to Bring the Baby

"Now when you say 'bring the baby,' do you mean actually *bring* the baby, or do you mean it in more of a metaphorical sense?"

"What baby?"

"Oh my gosh, I'd love to see her! I mean the party's proba- bly going to go a little late, and there won't be any other kids there, but that'll just make her more special, and remember nothing is baby-proofed, so we'll want to keep an eye on her, and there are a lot of antiques—you don't want to even know the replacement cost of that stuff—and of course we'll keep her away from the boa constrictor . . . oh, are you sure? Because I'd really love to see her."

Parties Are Such Sweet Sorrow

If you do bring your baby to a party, one thing you will have to address is the **inevitable crying fit.** While they cannot be avoided, tantrums at parties can at least be contained if the reasons for them are properly understood.

It's Your Party and I'll Cry If . . .

I'm tired.

I'm offered a bite of cheddar but would prefer goat cheese.

My diaper is wet.

Somone's facial expression irks me.

I feel the conversation needs a little "shot in the arm."

The Big Spill

There will of course be a variety of small spills to contend with, but at some point there is also the chance that your child will create a **category 5 spill**—a legendary spill, a spill everyone will remember. Category 5 spills can either be quick and decisive (a glass of red wine all over a white blouse, for example) or slow building yet inexorable (i.e., a chain-reaction spill involving a thrown toy, a candelabra, a bowl of guacamole, and a light-colored carpet).

If your child causes a category 5 spill, the first thing you should do is **sprinkle salt or baking soda on the area of the spill.** This does nothing to remove the stain, but does make for a comforting ritual. After this, the most important thing is to **apologize profusely** for the mess.

THE PROFUSE APOLOGY

Profuse apologies differ from normal apologies in both length and content. A normal apology might sound something like, "I'm so sorry." A profuse apology, on the other hand, generally requires that the "sorry" be modified by a stronger word than *so:* "monumentally sorry," "hopelessly sorry," and "stratospherically sorry" are all good examples of profuse apology hyperbole.

Furthermore, the initial "sorry" clause should be immediately followed by an offer of reparations: "Let me clean that for you," "I'll pay for that," and "You may strike me if you wish" are all appropriately profuse follow-ups to the original apology.

RESTAURANTS

The nice thing about gatherings in restaurants is that, unlike private homes, you are generally not liable for the damage inflicted. In fact, assuming the restaurant is appropriate for children, spills and other havoc may pass largely unnoticed. The real question is how to know if a restaurant is child appropriate.

THE RESTAURANT IS APPROPRIATE FOR CHILDREN IF:

The waiters are wearing headgear of any kind.
The words "Pancake" or "Bob" appear anywhere in the title of the restaurant.
There is a glass-encased pie rotisserie.
The buffet is protected by a sneeze screen.
The menu has pictures of food on it.
There is a vaguely fetid underlying odor, as though of a small animal decaying.

Eating in Front of Others

Once you've chosen a child-appropriate restaurant, all that remains is the issue of public eating etiquette. The specific rules may differ from place to place, but avoiding the following **universal dining faux pas** should help to ensure that you don't offend other diners.

Don't:

Eat food off of your baby's face.
Encourage the throwing of food, even if you are impressed
by the baby's arm strength.
Use that bulb syringe to suck mucus from the baby's nose.
Let your child visit other tables, expecting random diners to
find your child as charming as you do.
Change a diaper at the table.

ETIQUETTE TIP

It is appropriate to add ten percent to your tip for every
entrée that ends up on the floor. For every entrée that strikes
the actual waitperson, a twenty percent increase is standard.

WEDDINGS

Weddings can be very confusing when it comes to bringing a
baby. Some people view weddings as the ultimate family event
and believe children are a blessing upon the future couple;
others see weddings as ritzy adults-only parties that would be
marred by a shrieking infant. As with any gathering, it is always
good policy to begin by asking whether or not it is okay to bring
the baby.

FRIENDS AND FAMILY BOX

Why You Don't Want Children at Your Wedding

As a bride, there are a number of reasons you may not want young children at your wedding. The noise, distraction, and potential messes can all be galling but ultimately are nothing compared to the fact that **photographers are obsessed with small children** (see figures 1 and 2). If you don't want your wedding album to turn into an Anne Geddes retrospective, politely ask in your invitations that children be left at home.

First dance picture without children.

First dance picture with children.

If Your Toddler Is the Flower Girl

In general, very young flower girls have only three essential duties.

First, she should look utterly adorable (if hairless, flower wreaths can work wonders).

Second, she should commit some directional error while toddling down the aisle (i.e., veering away from the altar and running toward mom or dad) that makes everyone in the audience chuckle.

Third, she should pose for a trite photo op with the ring bearer, perhaps kissing him on the cheek while onlookers say "awww" and try to appear genuinely touched.

A WEDDING TROUBLE-SHOOTING GUIDE FOR NEW PARENTS

Problem: Child shrieks during a particularly solemn moment.

Solution: Pretend it was not your child. Scowl in the direction of another child. Except for the people in your immediate vicinity, most guests will be fooled if you've picked out the proper scapegoat.

Problem: Your child vomits on a member of the wedding party.

Solution: Find some club soda. Pour the club soda into a glass with four to six ounces of vodka. Drink rapidly. Now that you've taken the edge off, you can start figuring out how to remove that stain.

Problem: Your child runs down the aisle during ceremony (but is not the flower girl).

Solution: Run after her. When you catch her, return to your seat doing a wincing, slinking "Scooby-Doo" tiptoe, as if that will make the whole thing less obtrusive.

Problem: Your child throws a fit at the reception.

Solution: Administer *faux discipline* as you usher her outside. Loudly say something like, "Honey, we don't scream and throw things at other people's parties, that's not what we do." Use prominent hand movements and pretend that you are actually communicating with your child—remember, the point is to reassure onlookers that discipline is being administered.

Dancing with the Baby

No matter what else has gone wrong at the wedding, you have one final chance to make amends once the music starts to play. Take your baby to the dance floor, pick her up, and twirl her around as she laughs with delight. The sight of a daddy dancing with his infant daughter, or a mother with her son, has an almost magical power to soothe any feelings of ill will.

Who Gets to Get Drunk at the Reception?

Perhaps the most important question when taking your child to a wedding reception is deciding which parent gets to get drunk.

If one member of the couple is in the wedding party, it is usually a foregone conclusion that they are allowed to indulge.

If neither member is in the wedding party, the etiquette is usually to decide who got drunk the last time, and alternate accordingly.

If no one can remember who got to get drunk the last time, the best remaining option is to race. Whoever gets drunk first gets to stay drunk, while the other has to scale it back and act like a responsible parent.

CHURCH

Whether you are going for a christening, a funeral, or simply a normal Sunday service, the essential thing when taking your baby to church is praying to God that they don't humiliate you. Praying is of course good practice prior to any event but does seem particularly apropos for church ceremonies.

Sample prayers might include:

"Would you shut up, for Christ's sake?"

"Lord, lead us not into defecation."

"God, I don't ask for much, but if you could just adios that smell for the next thirty minutes or so, I'd totally appreciate it. Seriously, God, could you help a brother out? People are giving me dirty looks. Hey, they're not supposed to cast dirty looks in church, are they?"

"Let there be wipes!"

ETIQUETTE TIP

All of the advice in this chapter is of course moot
if you follow the number-one rule of
event etiquette—HIRE A BABY-SITTER!

15

Crib Notes

Education Etiquette

Baby Genius Training

When parents think about their child's education, they are usually worried about K–12 schooling and how to pay for college. Recently, however, new parents have been discovering the benefits of infant education through the many "Baby Genius" products and services that help promote a child's intellectual development right from the start.

Baby Einstein Videos

New parents are sometimes concerned that early exposure to television might be bad for their baby, but in the case of Baby Einstein videos they should not worry. These are, after all, Baby *Einstein* videos. Einstein was a genius, and they would not name the videos after him unless viewing them was also likely to make your child a genius. So pop in the video, sit back, and think about where you want to set that Nobel Prize.

Note: Anyone who enjoys the Baby Einstein series may also be interested in **Baby Kruschev,** for parents hoping to raise a politically savvy hard-liner, and **Baby Trump,** for anyone hoping to rear a wealthy narcissist. A new and particularly exciting series for aspiring infant poets is **Baby Plath,** with its award-winning "Daddy, I'm through" video.

Baby Educational Product FAQs

Q: If I don't buy a mobile with those shiny metal things that whirl around, will my child fall terribly behind other children developmentally?
A: Yes. Those shiny whirling metal things are essential to your child's early intellectual development, and without them there is little chance that she will get into the college of her choice.

Q: I've seen some commercials for baby language tapes that say children learn best when they're young. Should I be teaching my two-year-old foreign languages?
A: No. You should be teaching him not to poop himself. There will be plenty of time for advanced multilingualism after the whole potty thing is worked out.

Q: I know that reading to your child is important, but the repetition is killing me. If I have to read *The Runaway Bunny* one more time, I'm afraid I'll lose my mind. Is there any way out of rereading purgatory?
A: Yes. Start making up words to the story. Babies do not really know what you're saying, anyway, they just like you to

perform for them. So go ahead and substitute some slightly more adult content. For example:

"If you run after me," said the little bunny, "I will become a Baggie of illegal contraband smuggled across the border in the waistband of an overweight bandito."

"If you become a Baggie of illegal contraband smuggled across the border in the waistband of an overweight bandito," said his mother, "I will become a DEA agent who mows the bandito down in a hail of non-lethal rubber bullets and then seizes you as evidence."

LANGUAGE ETIQUETTE

It is a wondrous thing to watch babies learning language. They imitate everything you say, moving quickly from simple words like "mama" and "dada" to actual phrases like "I want it" and "Shut up, I hate you—God, you're so totally out of touch." Few things are as adorable as a fourteen-month-old mastering her first sentence. The downside of this process, however, is that babies learn by imitating *everything you say*.

It is one thing to know that it is inappropriate to swear in front of children and quite another to follow that rule yourself. You may reason that your child is eventually going to hear this stuff anyway, so they might as well hear it from you. This philosophy makes perfect sense until your baby drops her first public F-bomb.

When Your Child Swears in Public

When your child breaks out the F-word, and she will, the most important thing is that you do not panic. If you overreact—laughing, shrieking, hiding, or even shouting, "Honey, we don't say that!"—your child will know that this word is the way to produce a reaction, and it will become forever ingrained in her vocabulary. The only appropriate course of action here is very calmly to correct your child's "mispronunciation": "I'm sorry, honey, we didn't bring your fork. I think I have your spoon, though. Would you like your spoon?"

When Your Child Repeats What You Said Behind Someone's Back

Most people quickly learn to avoid swearing in front of children, but this is rarely the case with statements such as, "Brenda's really been getting fat." Children have fantastically long memories, and you can be sure that the next time you say, "Look who's here, honey, it's Aunt Brenda!" your child will say, "Getting fat!" Again, your best option in this situation is to go with the "mispronunciation" defense: "You're right, honey, Mommy did get a flat tire yesterday." "Nooo, Brenda fat!" "No, honey, Brenda didn't get the flat, Mommy did!" You will have to keep this argument up for as long as your child does.

PREPARING FOR PRESCHOOL

Getting into a good preschool is no easy task, and today's well-prepared parents begin planning their application strategy ahead of time. Part of this preparation will involve building your child's preschool résumé.

Extracurricular activities: Gymboree, Mommy and Me classes, music classes, and swim classes can all help to create that all-important "overachiever" image for your infant. The essential thing here is to overschedule your child, because this will show preschools that the baby is already prepared for the radical overscheduling that will occur once school, soccer practice, and play-dates are rolled into the mix around age four.

Volunteer work: You may feel that your infant is too young to engage in volunteer work, but remember from your own résumé-building experiences that "volunteer work" entries are rarely real. This is more the creative-writing part of the résumé. If the baby visits her great-grandmother in a nursing home, for instance, you should feel free to write down "Nursing home volunteer—Worked creating games and performing to cheer the elderly." In fact, you can go ahead and keep that on her résumé all the way through college.

Toddler groups: One excellent way to prepare for preschool is to enroll your child in a toddler group. Toddler groups are one of the first places you can begin to get objective feedback about your child and see what their academic personalities will be like relative to their peers. When discussing your child with the toddler teacher, remember that it is now fashionable for teachers to replace potentially derogative descriptions of toddlers with more positive characterizations. The following translation table should help you to communicate in the language of Toddler PC.

TODDLER PC TRANSLATION TABLE

Crybaby	substitute	Dramatic
Loud	substitute	Enthusiastic
Greedy, cruel	substitute	Businesslike
Demon spawn	substitute	Spirited
Obnoxious little #$%#	substitute	Strong-willed
Dishonest	substitute	Lawyerly
Inept at reading, speaking	substitute	Presidential

PICKING A PRESCHOOL

Parents sometimes get a bit overzealous about how much of an academic advantage a good preschool will give their child later on in life. While academics are always important, there are also other concerns when choosing your preschool.

WHAT PARENTS WORRY ABOUT	WHAT THEY SHOULD WORRY ABOUT
Whether school uses Piaget or Reggio Emilia methods.	Whether school contains asbestos, toxic mold, or scary poisonous spiders.
Whether teachers have masters degrees in early childhood education.	Whether teachers have sharp eyes and quick feet.
Whether your child will like their teacher.	Whether your child will like their teacher more than you.

DID YOU KNOW?

Children who are homeschooled realize that their parents are "dorks" an average of eighteen months later than children who attend public school. Children who attend private school are apparently born with this knowledge.

APPLYING TO PRESCHOOL

In today's world, the question of "affirmative action" is no longer just for higher education. With the recent baby boom, nearly everyone is having trouble getting into a good preschool, and if possible you should turn preschools' interest in acquiring a diverse student body to your advantage.

Looking for Diversity

RACE

Remember when filling out your application that diversity is important. In the box on "race," for instance, try not to check Caucasian. Even if your child is fully Caucasian, check the box marked "other," and then next to it write something like, "Although little Jeffrey is Caucasian, his cousin Blaine is 1/64 Native American. Through Blaine, Jeffrey has had many "non-white" experiences (hearing his Baby Bjorn called a "papoose," for example) that have taught him tolerance and have truly broadened him as a person."

PARENTS' SEXUAL ORIENTATION

Many of the most progressive preschools now consider the parents' sexual orientation among their diversity criteria. If either parent considers themselves to be gay, make sure to note this on the application form; if not, try to make the best of whatever experience you have in the "comments" section. Example: "Although we consider ourselves 'heterosexual,' Jennifer did have a brief, drunken encounter with a woman in college and remembers thinking it was fun."

Bribing Preschool Officials

If all else fails, you may want to consider attempting a bribe. While officials at universities, colleges, and private high schools are used to accepting bribes (in academic parlance, these are usually called "donations"), officials at preschools often do not have such a well-ordered system set up for the delivery of cash.

In such cases, it is generally good practice to place your "donation" in an unmarked envelope and then hand deliver it to the school's principal. Simply say you were "impressed" by the tour and would like to make a "contribution." As your child gets older, remember that this technique is also useful in terms of getting them into Ivy League universities and, if you so desire, the Texas Air National Guard.

FINDING OUT IF YOUR CHILD IS THE SMARTEST WITHOUT COMING OFF AS IMPERTINENT

Once your child is enrolled in a good preschool, the only thing you have left to worry about is whether or not she is the smartest and/or most talented toddler in her class.

When pumping a teacher for compliments about your child, the most important thing is to come off as modest and concerned rather than overbearing and competitive. "I'm a bit worried about her speaking skills—is she doing okay relative to the other students?" is a much more appropriate question, for instance, than, "What's her class rank?"

16

Let's Just Go
Travel Etiquette

AUTOMOBILE ETIQUETTE
Parentally Impaired Driving

Man or woman, young or middle-aged, it is inevitable that you will drive horrendously when you are a new parent. You will be exhausted, anxious, and distracted—in short, a nightmare for other drivers. Unfortunately, there is little you can do to control your miserable driving. What you can do, however, is publicly announce yourself as parentally impaired by driving a **minivan.**

Acquiring Your Minivan

Contrary to popular belief, there is no need to spend time comparing minivan models in terms of gas mileage or interior cargo space. It ultimately does not matter what make or model of minivan you buy, because they are all **exactly the same.** You can, however, retain some vestigial sense of individual identity through your choice of color.

Minivan Color Options:
  Gray beige
  Clay beige
  Classic beige
  Khaki

Note: some dealers also offer a "champagne beige" color option. Try to remember, though, that there is a difference between setting yourself subtly apart from the crowd and saying, "Hey, look at me, I'm driving a whole different shade of beige!"

PREPARING FOR DRIVING WITH CHILD IN CAR

Before you actually attempt to drive with a baby in the car, it is important to prepare yourself by simulating the experience as closely as possible. For example:

1) To practice driving **while watching your child instead of the road,** try reading a magazine or newspaper while behind the wheel.

2) To simulate driving under the duress of **periodic shrieking,** you can have your spouse sit in the backseat and scream or convulse at random intervals.

3) Later on, as your child nears the age (usually about one year) when the car seat is turned to face the front, you may also want to practice driving while being periodically pelted by **Cheerios and soft fruit.**

FRIENDS AND FAMILY BOX
Driving in the Car with a New Parent

Do not do it.

    Possible excuses may include:
Allergic to Enfamil
Might need to leave event early
Have to make a private cell-phone call
Don't want to die

    Do not feel guilty about saving yourself. Remember that when the crash does come, you will be able to help your friends instead of being incapacitated along with them.

The Baby Car Seat

Baby car seats are the law in all fifty states, and most maternity wards will not even allow you to depart with your child unless you can demonstrate that you already have a working car seat installed. It is thus a good idea to have the car seat in place **well before you leave for the hospital.** Since women in their third trimester of pregnancy are discouraged from performing manual labor, the job of installation will generally fall to the father-to-be.

The good news is that car seats come in only two pieces—
the "base" and the seat. Our easy-to-follow illustrated instructions will guide you smoothly through the installation process.

Car-Seat Installation Instructions

Step 1: Remove car seat and base from packaging.
Step 2: Wonder briefly why car seat and base do not even remotely resemble the pictures in the instruction manual (see figure 1).

Figure 1

Step 3: Attempt and fail to thread seat belt through base.

Step 4: Curse (see figure 2).

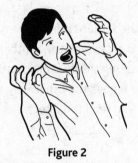

Figure 2

Step 5: Turn base around.

Step 6: Repeat steps 3–4.

Step 7: Call "manufacturer's help line" number listed on instructions.

Step 8: Wait on hold for several minutes before being disconnected.

Step 9: Return to car, where pregnant wife has successfully threaded seat belt through car-seat base (see figure 3).

Figure 3

Public Transportation

While we cannot in good conscience recommend public transportation as a way of transporting either yourself or your child, there is a good chance that you will at some point find yourself aboard either a bus or subway train.

The most important aspect of bus and subway etiquette is sitting next to someone sympathetic—this will help you to avoid conflict and even, with luck, find solace.

ETIQUETTE TIP
Do not assume that people are kindly or sympathetic simply because they are old.

The best way to find a sympathetic seat mate is to look directly into your fellow passengers' faces as you board the vehicle. Their expressions will likely fall into one of the following categories.

The look away: The look away, while not overtly aggressive, is a definite warning sign. As soon as your child begins acting out, this

The Look Away

person will most likely say, either to themselves or to a fellow passenger, "Best form of birth control there is." The fact that they are correct is immaterial. They are still mean and should be avoided.

The eye roll with mumble: The eye roll is not as dire as it may at first appear. Eye rollers are dramatic, narcissistic people who could be lured by your child as a potential audience. If the person makes an exasperated face and your child laughs or smiles, you may well find yourself with built-in entertainment for the remainder of the journey.

The Eye Roll With Mumble

The sympathetic half-smile (not to be confused with the ironic smirk): The sympathetic half-smile is the Holy Grail of travel companions. This kindly, weak-minded individ-

The Sympathetic Half-Smile

ual truly believes that children are our future; they will talk resolutely about their own offspring and will probably at some point offer your child some hard candy or stale chocolate.

The drug-induced stupor: Many new parents wrongly shy away from the drug-induced stupor, fearing that the "passed out" individual will revive and become troublesome or violent. While this does sometimes happen in movies, it is rarely the case in real life. In general, unconscious individuals are excellent travel companions and will do little more than groan and/or drool slightly even when your child grows restless and begins pelting them with arrowroot biscuits.

The Drug-Induced Stupor

Airplane Etiquette
The Screaming Baby

Babies often cry more on airplanes because their ears have trouble adjusting to pressure changes. When this happens, you have several potential courses of action.

1) Alleviate the child's suffering through bottle or breast-feeding. Repeated swallowing should help to equalize pressure in the ears, and this familiar and comforting activity will help the baby to calm down.

2) Pretend that the child is not yours. This works particularly well if you are a father traveling with your wife and child. When you see that the child is on the verge of a fit, excuse yourself to use the bathroom. Take along a magazine, lock yourself inside, and do not come out until the pilot announces that landing is imminent.

3) Feign dementia. Smile peacefully, as though wholly unaware that you are at the center of an irritation maelstrom.

The Diaper Check

While a "smell check" is both appropriate and considerate of your neighbors, the "finger check" is highly inappropriate in a confined public space. Indeed, the only acceptable reason for a finger check is if your seat mate has offended you in some way and you wish to obtain revenge without attacking them directly. In this case, wait until they are eating and you are reasonably sure your child is carrying a full-fecal package. Insert one or more fingers, and then bring them out in full view of your traveling companion. To really drive the point home, go ahead and check with your middle finger.

The In-Flight Diaper Change

On any flight longer than two hours, you will probably have to conduct at least one in-flight diaper change. You can either attempt to make the change in the lavatory or, if the FASTEN SEAT BELT sign is on (and it will be), right there in your seat.

Projectile Urination

In the event of projectile urination, be sure to hide your child before hiding yourself. Once the child is safely stowed beneath the seat, place your seat back in the full upright position. Lean forward and place your head between your knees (see figure 1). This position should shield you from the view of the offended passenger.

Figure 1

PACKING

When packing for a trip, the proper approach will differ depending on your gender.

Female: Whether the journey is long or short, make sure to pack everything your child owns. This should include clothes that are still too big, because it is not impossible that your little one will experience a growth spurt on the way to Gymboree. It is also vital that, before departing, you return at least twice to the house to retrieve seemingly irrelevant objects, such as sun-

---

FELLOW TRAVELER BOX
What to Do if a Child Is Kicking Your Seat

The key to this interaction is total commitment to passive-aggression. Rather than simply asking the child to stop, you should initiate a series of frustrated yet impotent gestures beginning with the **querulous half-turn.** When this fails to produce results, proceed to the **annoyed full turn with questioning glance,** as though you are wondering, "What could possibly be making my seat bounce in this exasperating way?" When both the child and parent ignore your full turn completely, it is time to proceed to a form of **passive-aggressive revenge.** Wait until food has been delivered to the table in back of your seat, then recline your seat back as forcefully and rapidly as possible. Repeat as necessary.

---

screen for an evening outing or a parka during a heat wave. Remember, it's not **OCD,** it's **mother's intuition.**

Male: Smile, carry bag after bag to the car, and don't say a word.

NONMOTORIZED BABY TRANSPORTATION
What your stroller says about you:

The "jogging" stroller says: You will not let "life challenges" such as parenthood come between you and your superficial appearance. Simultaneously more expensive and less functional than traditional strollers, jogging strollers are the BMWs of nonmotorized baby transportation.

The bicycle stroller attachment says: You are not afraid to "rough it," exposing your child early on to some of life's harsher elements. As you pedal bravely forth amidst throngs of ill-driven SUVs and minivans, remember that fresh air, exercise, and massive head trauma can all build character for the years to come.

The "double" or "triple" stroller says: Those fertility drugs really paid off. Good luck making college payments.

17

It's All Relative
Family Etiquette

"Home" Away from Home
The End of Holiday Travel?

One of the things new parents most look forward to is escaping the need to fly home for the holidays. No more overcrowded airports, no more weather delays, no more frequent-flying attempts to placate both sets of in-laws. The new baby, you reason, means that your house is now **home base,** and anyone who wants a visit will have to come to you. Sadly, this is rarely the case. The minute you suggest that traveling across the country with a young infant would be prohibitively difficult, grandparents will most likely come down with some condition that, while making it impossible for them to travel, would still allow them enough energy and mobility to play holiday host. Such conditions may include eye trouble, foot trouble, and disorders of the ever-mysterious "gall bladder."

Using "Ear Infections" to Get Out of Air Travel

Although babies cannot always make people come to you, they can definitely excuse you from having to fly anywhere else. Indeed, the whole point of "ear infections" is that they make flying impossible. This simple expedient will allow you and your spouse to spend some holiday alone time while simultaneously collecting family sympathy for your child's suffering.

D I D   Y O U   K N O W ?
72 percent of infant "ear infections" occur immediately prior to undesirable Thanksgiving, Christmas, or Memorial Day air travel.

Too Close for Comfort

If your relatives live too nearby for you to use an air-travel excuse, there is still a very simple way to avoid spending holidays away from home: The next time you visit your relatives' house, do nothing. Nothing whatsoever. Don't stop your child from running, screaming, throwing food, or **pulling pottery off of shelves.** Smile placidly when they yank the cat's tail or funnel apple juice into the VCR. If your relatives comment on your lack of parental control, calmly explain to them that you don't believe in "discipline" because it stifles creativity. The next time you are invited back to their house will be for your child's wedding shower.

WHEN YOUR RELATIVES VISIT YOU

The Difference Between Helpful and "Helpful"

One of the keys to getting along with visiting relatives is understanding their attempts to be "helpful." Do not confuse this with an attempt to be helpful. Being helpful would involve doing something that you actually need done when you need it done. Instead of this, your relatives will respond to needs that they either hope you have or think you should have. They may make you an elaborate breakfast, for instance, reasoning that you need to eat something. Then, when they discover you've already eaten, they will "helpfully" wolf the food down themselves. You will of course be responsible for the dishes.

THE MOTHER-IN-LAW COMMUNICATION GAP

There is often a communication gap that occurs between new parents and their in-laws, especially on the female side. You should try to understand that what your mother-in-law says is not always what you hear and, furthermore, not always what she actually means. The following table is meant as a kind of guide for new parents attempting to navigate an in-law conversation.

WHAT A MOTHER-IN-LAW SAYS	WHAT A NEW MOM HEARS	WHAT THE MOTHER-IN-LAW REALLY MEANS
Hello.	You're a bad mother.	Hello.

What a Mother-in-Law says	What a New Mom hears	What the Mother-in-Law Really Means
How are you feeling?	How are you feeling?	When I was your age, I cleaned, cut coupons, took care of three kids, and had dinner on the table at 6 P.M. every evening no matter how I was feeling. Feelings were for poets and crazy people, but now everyone's seeing a psychologist, and what, they're going to blame all their problems on their parents? I have some feelings about that, let me tell you . . .
Would you like me to do a little vacuuming?	How could my son have married such a slovenly cow?	How could my son have married such a slovenly cow?
Can I hold him?	You're not holding him right.	You're not holding him right, you slovenly cow.

What a Father-in-Law says	What a New Dad Hears	What a Father-in-Law Means
Beer?	Beer?	Beer?

FRIENDS AND FAMILY BOX
A Grandparent's Guide to the Gadgets

It is often difficult for grandparents to master baby-related technology that did not exist back when they were new parents. The following instructions should help grandparents navigate some of the more mystifying devices.

The "baby-proofed" toilet: Baby-proofed toilets are virtually impossible to open. Your best bet is probably to hold it until your son or daughter gets home (see figure 1).

Figure 1

The "Baby Bjorn": Using a "Baby Bjorn" carrying device is a three-step process, and it is essential that you take it one step at a time. **First,** untangle the various belts and pouches. **Second,** attempt to wrap, snap, and buckle the Bjorn into place on your body. **Third,** abandon the Bjorn and carry the baby in your arms like any normal person.

The baby gate: The trick to opening a baby gate is to **use both hands.** Put one hand on each side of the locking mechanism and squeeze. Squeeze hard. It is possible that skin from one or both index fingers will be ripped off by the mechanism as it opens, but at least you will be through the gate.

A drawer or cabinet "baby-proofed" with plastic depressors: Pull open the cabinet until the plastic latch catches (about a half-inch). Reach a finger in and press down on the plastic depressor, which will release the latch, and then open the drawer.

A drawer or cabinet "baby-proofed" with metal hinges and a sliding magnetic "opener": You cannot open this cabinet. No one can. Not even the people who installed it.

The baby monitor: After parents leave, turn switch to "off" position so that you don't have to listen to the baby toss, turn, and squawk all evening. Make sure to turn monitor back to "on" position before they get home.

WHAT ARE YOU SO WORRIED ABOUT?

New parents often worry about leaving their child in the care of someone else, even a grandparent. Grandparents, on the other hand, are often eager to baby-sit—both to spend time with the baby and also in the wildly optimistic hope that your spousal "alone time" will result in yet another grandchild. The resultant debates can sometimes be quite contentious, but the following examples should provide you with some helpful guidance as to which arguments you will win and which you will lose.

Your concern: Grandparents will leave the baby gate open and your baby could fall down the stairs.

Your parents' argument: Those baby gates are a fire hazard. Besides, you fell down the stairs a few times as a youngster and look how well you turned out.

Your rebuttal: Joey fell down the stairs, too, and look how *he* turned out!

The result: You win. Falling down stairs is never a good thing.

Your concern: Grandparents might leave bottle in the bottle warmer too long, and it's essential that her bottle be the exact right temperature.

Your parents' argument: You're being neurotic and controlling.

Your rebuttal: No, I'm not.

The result: Yes, you are. And you seriously need a night out on the town. They win.

Your concern: Grandparents won't follow the baby's normal bedtime ritual.

Your parents' argument: So what?

Your rebuttal: So, if she doesn't get to sleep the right way, she won't stay asleep, and then we'll be dealing with a crying baby in the middle of the night.

The result: This is a close call, but they win. Chances are you'll be dealing with a crying baby in the middle of the night no matter what anyone does.

Your concern: Grandparents might lock child in a footlocker the way they did to you.

Your parents' argument: That wasn't a footlocker, it was a small animal cage.

Your rebuttal: You're horrible people.

The result: This is tragic and dysfunctional. No one wins.

ETIQUETTE TIP
It is good baby etiquette to recognize
that you are to your parents what your
child is to you, and apologize.

FRIENDS AND FAMILY BOX
Sisters
*How to Deal with All the Attention Your Sister Is Getting
Just Because She Had a Baby and You Didn't*

If your sister has recently given birth but you remain childless and/or single, you will need to accept the fact that she is now far above you on the "approval hierarchy" set up by your parents. There are, however, certain time-tested rhetorical strategies that may help you feel better.

Faux humility: "Oh, me? Not much, I've been working on this thirty-seven-million-dollar arbitrage deal in preparation for a hostile takeover bid. I mean, it's nothing like what you go through with the diapers and everything, but it's been a pretty intense week."

Excuse with hopeful projection: "Ron's really focused on his career right now, but as soon as the whole job search bears fruit, we're going to have four kids, one named after each grandparent."

The hard truth: "The amazing thing about reproduction is that all animals do it."

FAMILY PETS

Cats

Cats are essentially a baby substitute for childless twenty- and thirty-something women, so when an actual baby arrives, the felines become superfluous. The same women who used to talk to their cats, groom them, carry them around, and even sleep in the same bed with them now have almost no memory that there was ever such a connection—it is as though they have broken up with the cat and moved on to a more fulfilling relationship. Cat boxes go uncleaned, meows go unanswered, plaintive "play with me" gestures go callously unattended. It is little wonder, then, that people with cats have a higher incidence of "accidents" than people without cats. It is probably best either to get your cat a friend or give him to someone without a baby.

Dogs

Dogs, while needy, can also be very useful in lapping up any and all food that gets spilled or thrown on the floor. Dogs also provide beleaguered husbands with an excellent excuse to get out of the house; all you have to do is take the dog for "a walk." If anyone asks why the dog smells like beer and cigarettes upon your return, simply reply that "he must have rolled in something."

18

The Lone Changer

Single-Parent Etiquette

DADDY DEAREST

The vast majority of single parents are moms, and the majority of this chapter will be devoted to their concerns. There are also, however, some single dads out there whose etiquette concerns should not go unnoticed. Our society tends to assume that men are not equal to women when it comes to parenting young children—not as capable of surviving without sleep, organizing shopping lists, changing diapers, and preparing dinner all at the same time. This prejudice is out there primarily because it is true. The average man in charge of a young infant is going to need some serious female help.

The Madonna/Poor Complex

If you do not have enough money to hire full-time help, you will probably want to befriend and/or date someone with a strong maternal instinct. The first step to doing this, of course, is learning to recognize a "Madonna" when you see one.

*Characteristics of Someone with a
Strong Maternal Instinct*

Cries during telephone commercials/animated features
Affinity for the three Cs: cats, candles, and Capri pants
Occasionally uses the phrase "soul mate" unironically
Occasionally uses the word "God" nonorgasmically
Carries food, tissues, and/or other noncosmetic items in
    purse
Is nice

FRIENDS AND FAMILY BOX

Signs That He Just Wants You for Your Mothering Skills

Seems grateful rather than suspicious of the nice things you do
Introduces you to his mother/sisters on or before third date
Has *Sleepless in Seattle* playing on TiVo whenever you come
    over
Answers questions about himself with candor
Says you look "so beautiful" when you change diapers
Mistily refers to "Itsy Bitsy Spider" as "our song"
Genuinely pretends to care about your dreams/fears

Hey, Baby . . .

Once you have identified someone you would like to date or befriend, you still have to meet and/or impress her. Some men believe that babies are a hindrance to meeting women, but this is false: Small children are to today's dating scene what adorable dogs used to be—attention-catching accoutrements that say, "I'm a sensitive, approachable straight guy." Either gender will suffice in terms of getting you an introduction, but if your child is a girl, you get the added opportunity to showcase the way you treat women. Dress your daughter up in designer outfits, have her hair done, carry her around on your shoulders, and buy her whatever she wants, and it won't be long before you are besieged by women vying for their own chance at landing the "sugar daddy" (see figure 1). The rest of the job is, as they say, like taking candy from a baby.

Figure 1

THE SINGLE MOM

There is a prevailing myth in our society that all single moms are widows, divorcées, or young women who've had an unplanned pregnancy. Increasingly often, however, single motherhood is simply a choice made by women who want to have a child and don't feel like waiting around for some mythical "Mr. Right." If this is the case for you, you will need to go through the tricky business of finding an appropriate *sperm donor*.

Avoiding the Bad Seed

Searching for donors can be an uncomfortable process, which is why some women elect the anonymity of a sperm bank.

THE SPERM BANK

The idea behind sperm banks is that you can pick out a list of attributes—height, hair color, eye color, etc.—that you would like your child to have. You can also supposedly choose IQ range, personality type, and other such characteristics that, in reality, may or may not be valid. Remember that many sperm donors are paid according to how desirable their traits are, so there is little incentive for actual honesty.

DID YOU KNOW?
The one personality trait you can be sure
all anonymous sperm donors possess is a willingness
to masturbate into a cup for money.

A FRIEND OR ACQUAINTANCE

In light of the above, an increasingly common tactic for aspiring single moms is to "borrow" the seed of a friend or acquaintance. This will give you a much more secure sense of what you are getting genetically. One mistake commonly made by women taking this approach, however, is choosing too intelligent a friend in their quest for "the perfect child." The last thing a single mom wants on her hands is too smart a child: They are difficult to handle when young and will completely dismiss you when they get older. A better choice than friends with M.D.s or Ph.D.s might thus be an out-of-work actor. Attractive, genial, and just dopey enough to take direction—that's the recipe for a "perfect" child.

D I D   Y O U   K N O W ?
Your kids are totally going to owe you when they grow up.

Asking for Help Under the Guise of a Friendly Offer

Single moms sometimes need help, and sometimes they're too proud to ask for it. Even if you don't want to ask overtly, though, you can always solicit help under the guise of making a friendly offer. The key to this strategy is understanding how to ask for what you want without really asking for it. The following table should help you to understand the process.

WHAT A SINGLE MOM SAYS	WHAT SHE ACTUALLY MEANS
"Bradley and I want to make you a birthday dinner."	"I'm hoping you'll watch Bradley while I get drunk in the kitchen and undercook a casserole."
"Would you like to come trick-or-treating with us?"	"I know you're dying for an excuse to binge on chocolate—I'm handing you one for the bargain price of two hours' baby-sitting."
"It's so much easier if you get a little practice before having one yourself."	"You're invited to participate in my 'scared celibate' program."
"Come on over, we're dying Easter eggs!"	"I'm exhausted and my house is trashed. Would you like to indulge your arts-and-crafts inclinations for an hour or so while I take a nap?"

What to Say When Someone Asks About Your "Husband"

Single moms will occasionally run into situations in which another mom asks about your "husband." Their curiosity is rarely malicious, but it does put you in the awkward position of being asked to reveal something about your personal life to a stranger. There are many ways to respond in such situations, and several of the most popular approaches are listed below:

Overly forthcoming "I wouldn't call him a husband. More like a sperm donor with sleepover privileges—which, by the way, have now been revoked . . ."

Fictional "Well, don't tell anyone . . . he's actually a spy. Sometimes he's undercover for years at a time. In fact, I'm not even sure he's my husband."

Crazy, threatening Stark silence and a hard, unwavering glare.

Ironic, Disneyesque "Somewhere out there, beneath the pale moonlight . . ."

Fashion conscious "I think husbands are very last year."

BABY LOVE

No matter how successful and self-sufficient you are, no matter how great a mom you are to your child, there will at some point be someone who suggests that you need to "find yourself a man." You should feel free to ignore this person. If you do choose to participate in a discussion about why you are single, however, you may find it useful to have at your disposal some solid facts about why **babies are better than men.** Even happily married moms feel like single moms a lot of the time, and it is probably a good idea for all women—married or single—to keep the following list in mind when the mothering gets tough. You can't leave those babies, after all, so you might as well love them.

TOP TEN REASONS BABIES ARE BETTER THAN MEN

1. Both make a mess when they go #1, but at least babies don't leave the seat up.
2. Babies let you dress them in pastels.
3. When babies are upset, they cry instead of making subtly passive-aggressive comments that eat slowly but surely away at your sense of self-worth.
4. Babies like to cuddle.
5. When babies have gas, you can release it by patting their back instead of pulling their finger.
6. When babies say "I love you," they sometimes mean it.
7. Babies actually do give you a headache—no need to pretend.
8. Babies don't let baldness affect their self-esteem.
9. Babies don't go out for drinks with "friends" from the office, then stumble in at 2 A.M. reeking of some cheap floozy.
10. One day, babies stop being babies—men never stop being babies.

CONCLUSION
It Goes By So Fast

The parting comment you will hear most often from experienced parents is, "Enjoy it—it goes by so fast." *So fast compared to what?* you may wonder, as one long day blends into yet another long, sleepless night, becoming a single stretch of time that continues seemingly without end.

The truth is that the "so" in "so fast" is actually a special parental modifier that negates the meaning of whatever it precedes. Because of its unmatched versatility, "so" can be useful in almost any situation that requires good-natured insincerity. Wondering how to respond when you run into parents you've been avoiding since Lamaze class? Try "It's so good to see you!" Not sure what to say about someone else's child? "He's getting so big!" always works in a pinch.

That said, though, you should try whenever possible to avoid throwaway "so's" such as "so cute" and "so smart," and save them instead for more important fabrications such as "so happy," "so rewarding," and, of course, "so fast." The trick with "so's," as with all parental clichés, is to maintain the illusion of genuine discourse by avoiding overuse.

If, in the end, you can purge even a few unnecessary "so's" from your daily conversation, you will have put some sincerity back in parental conversation and taken at least one very valuable lesson from this book.

Which, by the way, thank you so much for reading!

Also from Adam Wasson and Jessica Stamen

The Self-Destruction Handbook
1-4000-5033-2
$12.00

Let's face it, there are thousands of books out there to help you avoid
self-destructive behavior—but what fun is that? Welcome to the first book
designed to help you not help yourself. Here you'll find unsound advice
on everything from engineering a revenge affair to picking
the gateway drug that's best for you.

> Chapters include
> • 12 Steps to a Drinking "Problem"
> • Condoms Are for Suckers
> • How to Lose Way Too Much Weight in 90 Days
> And more!

As you travel down the road to self-destruction, let this hedonistic
handbook be your guide. It may steer you wrong—in fact, it's sure to do
so—but when being wrong is this much fun, who wants to be right?